RED · GUIDE

DEVON

MARTYN BROWN

Oh! the little maids of Devon,
They have skins of milk and cream,
Just as pure and clear and even
As a pool in a Dartmoor stream,
But who looks at them is holden
With the magic of a dream.

DOROTHY FRANCIS GURNEY

RED GUIDE

DEVON

MARTYN BROWN

TO JANE, HARRIET AND PETER

AUTHOR
Martyn Brown

ILLUSTRATOR
Mark Peppé

COVER ILLUSTRATION
Glyn Dawson

EDITING
First Edition

TOWN INFORMATION PANELS
Vijay Patel; additional work by Virginia Langer

CARTOGRAPHY
© *The Automobile Association 1989*

Typeset by
Avonset, Midsomer Norton, Bath

Printed and bound by
Richard Clay Limited, Bungay,
Suffolk

The contents of this publication
are believed correct at the time of
printing. Nevertheless, the
Publishers cannot accept
responsibility for errors or
omissions, nor for changes in
details given.

Published by
Waymark Publications,
an imprint of The
Automobile Association

© The Automobile Association 1989

Produced and distributed in the
United Kingdom by the
Publishing Division of
The Automobile Association,
Fanum House, Basingstoke,
Hampshire RG21 2EA

ISBN 0 86145 807 9

HOW TO USE THIS BOOK

The *Red Guide Devon* divides the county into six sections.
These sections are divided again into smaller areas to explore.
Most of the smaller areas begin with a description of the largest
town, or another good place to start a tour. This is followed by
an exploration of the surrounding area.

The map on pages 6–7 shows starting points for local tours,
with page numbers.

A complete, alphabetical list of all the places in the book is
given in the index at the end of the book, together with details
of other towns in the county.

Town information panels
Practical information is given for selected towns. This includes
early closing and market days, cashpoints, tourist information
centres, places to visit, leisure centres, cinemas, and access by
road and rail. Places to visit which are closed for much of the
year, or which only open on a few days of the week are
marked *. At the time of going to press, places not marked with
an asterisk were open all year round, and on most days of the
week. Tourist information centres will have details of any
changes.

For information on places mentioned
elsewhere in the book, contact local
tourist information offices, or the
regional tourist board:
West Country Tourist Board,
37 Southernhay East, Exeter,
Devon EX1 1QS.

Or see The Automobile Association's
annual guide to places to visit in
Britain.

Other useful addresses:
Devon Wildlife Trust, 35 New Bridge
Street, Exeter,
Devon EX3 4AH.

English Heritage, 23 Savile Row,
London W1X 2BT

National Trust,
36 Queen Anne's Gate,
London SW1H 9AS

National Gardens Scheme
(private gardens opened occasionally
to the public),
57 Lower Belgrave Street,
London SW1W 0LR.
Annual booklet available in shops
in spring.

Royal Society for Protection of Birds
(RSPB), The Lodge, Sandy,
Beds SG19 2DL

Royal Society for Nature Conservation
(RSNC),
The Green, Nettleham,
Lincoln LN2 2NR

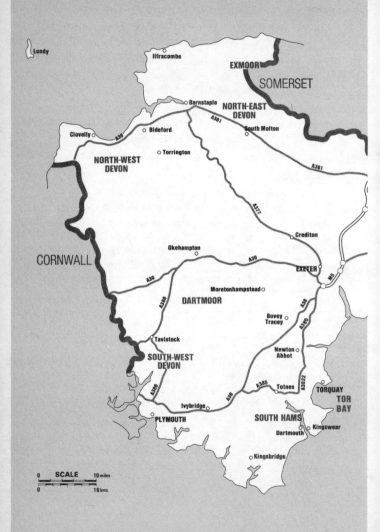

CONTENTS

M5

DORSET

A303

A30   A35   Axminster

SOUTH-EAST
DEVON

Budleigh
Salterton

INTRODUCTION

THE MOST POPULAR image of Devon as a holiday destination is epitomised in the promotion of Torbay as the English Riviera; posters create an image of a subtropical palm-waving paradise with perpetually blue skies and apparently warm seas. Without doubt it is this area of Devon, from the Exe estuary southwards to Dartmouth and Kingsbridge, and including the Mecca of Torbay, that attracts the majority of the summer visitors, but this image masks the tranquillity and charm of much of the county and belies its rich variety.

A contrasting view of the county might emphasise the fiery red soils of south-east Devon, matching the herds of Devon red cattle, cider from a stoneware flask in an orchard of trees bent low under the heavy crop of fruit; black faced shaggy sheep seeking the shelter of roadside ditches; hedges plastered in primroses; and winters of deep snow that cuts off farms for days on end.

Of course Devon is changing fast as motorway extensions probe towards Plymouth, Barnstaple and Okehampton, and London commuters can take the high-speed train from Exeter to reach the city in a little over two hours or even faster. Exeter itself is home to high-tech and promotes itself to international business as a convenient location in a desirable area.

Such changes have brought newcomers to Devon – not just those seeking a quiet retirement retreat, but young people and families living and working in the county and well aware of their good fortune in finding such a pleasant environment.

Much of the landscape has altered little since Daniel Defoe and other travellers first extolled its virtues; Dartmoor, once rejected as a barren wilderness and waste, now demands careful management as its open spaces attract such numbers as to threaten the very qualities those visitors come to enjoy. The coasts have suffered the usual rashes of development, chalets and caravan parks except where protected by the National Trust and the South West Heritage Coast; and yet despite this press of people on the limited natural resources of space there remain great tracts of wild country, of deserted footpaths, of windswept cliff-top paths where hikers and walkers can ramble for miles with scarcely another soul in sight.

In deepest rural Devon, where the narrow lanes, banked on either side by high hedges, wander crooked through the patchwork of hopelessly uneconomic tiny fields, country life continues. The Beaford Centre archive and the outstanding photographs of James Ravilious record a way of life for country people that is scarcely touched by modern trappings. Lean on a gate almost anywhere and the chances are a passer-by will join you to reminisce. In Devon people seem to have time – and, if anything, it is the people who make the county special and distinguish it from everywhere else in southern England. The rich warm brogue of the Devonshire dialect may be dying out, but the hospitality and kindness of the people remains a living tradition.

The *Red Guide – Devon* divides the county into six regions of approximately equal size; they may be pictured as five segments of a wheel around the central hub of Dartmoor. Though merging at the edges, each region is distinguished by the particular characteristics of its geography. Within each region, following the identification and description of principal centres, there are recommended tours – to small towns, villages, hamlets, museums, country houses and suggestions for walks or further exploration.

In addition, side panels draw attention to some of the most interesting individual sites, customs and folklore.

ACKNOWLEDGEMENTS

' 'Tis an account of places and things from inspections, not compiled from others' labours, or travels in one's study' – William Stukeley, *Itinerarium Curiosum*, 1776.

The pleasure of preparing this book has been the opportunity afforded to travel and retravel the back lanes and byways of Devon; I have been greatly assisted by my family, and particularly by my sister Louise who, together with Robert Watson, has contributed much time and effort to assist with typing and editing skills – to them, and Jessie and Emily, my sincere thanks.

MARTYN BROWN

Exeter

Population: 91,938

Market Days: Mon to Sat

Cashpoints: *Barclays* 20 High St; *Lloyds* 234 High St, Sowton Industrial Estate; *Midland* 38 High St, 9 St Thomas Centre Cowick St; *NatWest* The Castle 246 High St, 18 St Thomas Centre Cowick St

Tourist Information: Civic Centre, Paris St; Exeter Service Area (M5), Jct 30, Sandy Gate

Attractions: Devonshire Regiment Museum, Exeter Cathedral, Quay House Interpretation Centre, Guildhall, Maritime Museum, Rougemont House Museum, Royal Albert Memorial Museum, St Nicholas' Priory, Tuckers Hall*, Underground Passages

Arts: Barnfield Theatre, Exeter and Devon Arts Centre, Northcott Theatre

Leisure: Clifton Hill Sports Centre, The Plaza, St Peter's Community Sports Hall

Cinemas: Odeon Film Centre

By Road: London 170 miles (M5, M4), Okehampton 25 miles (A30), Plymouth 44 miles (A38)

By Rail: 2hrs 15mins from London (London, Paddington to Penzance line) and some faster services. Direct services to Barnstaple, Exmouth and Newton Abbot.

1 Exeter and South-East Devon

The Exe estuary, and the settlement on the bluff overlooking the river at the lowest fording place, for generations marked the limits of civilisation; beyond lay the wilds and the barbarians. A great Roman road drove straight and confident from Honiton to Isca, the Romans' name for Exeter, but west of the city it fizzled out; the Fosse Way, with a branch to the port of Axmouth, stretches north and east towards the Midlands, with barely a deviation on its way.

South-east Devon is a humpy landscape of broad river valleys leading from the Blackdown Hills in the north, which form the frontier with Somerset, to the south coast. The Axe, the Sid and the Otter have carved the high cliffs into bays of coarse shingle; once, at the mouths of each river there were busy ports, but now each is barricaded by a ridge of pebbles cast up by the sea.

There is no sand on the beaches between Exmouth and West Bay (Dorset). Fierce erosion by the sea has created landslips at Branscombe and Axmouth as impressive as those at Lyme Regis – at Branscombe, chalk pinnacles peer above the tangle of undergrowth where the undercliff creates a sheltered wilderness of a valley backed by raw-edged cliff. From Sidmouth westward the cliffs change from white to pink to red, the ruddy red sandstone familiar to every train traveller beyond Exeter where the track flashes in and out of tunnels in the red cliffs and crashed rocks stain the sea a gruesome hue, as the rhyme says:

It's certainly odd that this part of the coast,
While neighbouring Dorset gleams like a ghost,
Should look like anchovy sauce spread on toast.
'The Monk of Haldon' by R H D Barham

Inland the scene is of verdant pasture fringed
with thick hedges of hawthorn and ash, the
valley bottoms misty on fine mornings, with
the hills touched by the sun sparkling and fresh.

Daniel Defoe described the Otter valley at
Honiton as 'the most beautiful landskip in the
world, a mere picture; and I do not remember
the like in any one place in England.' The
valley has not changed much; although the
towns have expanded and suburbia bitten into
the field pattern.

The area is rich in archaeology, with hill-
forts at Hembury, Blackbury, Sidbury and
Woodbury. The forts dominate the valleys and
the transport routes. The pattern of later
settlement follows the topography with
principal towns – Exeter, Axminster, Honiton,
Ottery St Mary – at the river crossings;
elsewhere a thin scatter of villages and hamlets
with outlying farms. Exeter is the focus of the
transport network with main roads, motorway
(M5) and railway converging at the lowest
crossing point of the Exe; distant memories of
the annual traffic jams on the infamous Exeter
bypass will never fade. The pleasant settings
and mild climate of Exmouth and Sidmouth
attracted visitors as early as the 18th century;
the other resorts soon proclaimed their
attributes and Budleigh Salterton, Seaton and
Beer followed as fashions and transport
developed and the seaside holiday became a
national institution. Today each seaside town
retains much of its original style – none has
been overwhelmed by gross modern
developments and they remain places of
considerable charm. The focal point of the
region, however, is Exeter, where this chapter
begins.

Exeter Cathedral

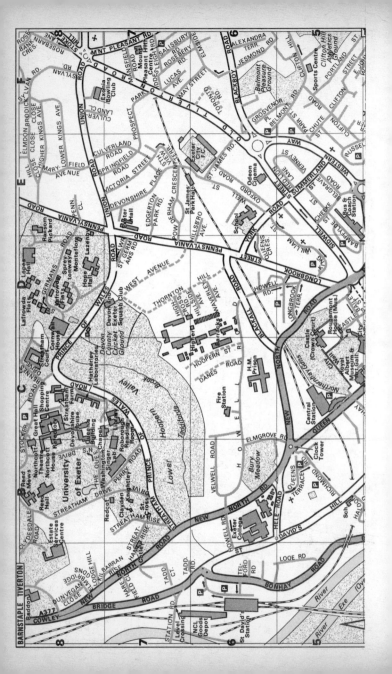

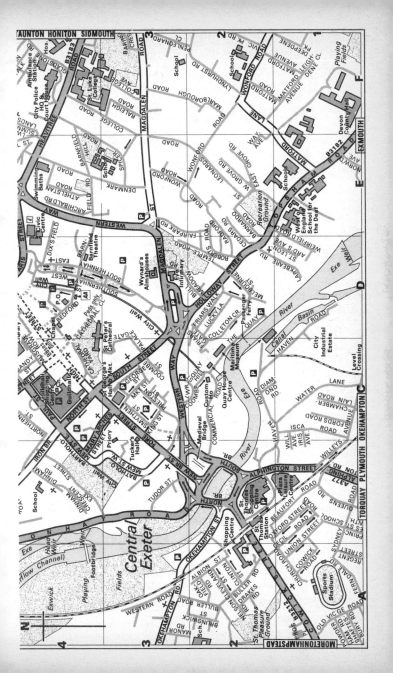

EXETER

The county capital and mother-city of south-western England, modern **Exeter** is the thriving administrative and cultural centre for the region.

The Cathedral Close frames the great church miraculously saved from the bombs which destroyed so much of the city during the last war. But the present building, ancient though it is, overlies still earlier foundations – Vespasian, the Roman general who imposed a grid-iron town plan on the plateau 100ft above the lowest ford across the river, found a Celtic tribe settled here, the Dumnonii, after whom Devon is named. Directly beside the west front, the main entrance to the Cathedral excavations in 1970 revealed the remains of the Roman bath-house – they have been filled in temporarily to await a contentious scheme for development as an attraction.

The Cathedral dates from 1050, when Bishop Leofric transferred his see from Crediton to Exeter to benefit from the protection of the walled city; elements of the Norman Cathedral still survive and are clearly visible in the round-headed blind arches of the north tower, but the present building dates predominantly from the 14th century.

The beauty of the nave is breathtaking – the great breadth and length, the rich windows and the uniformity of the architecture. The vaulting and clustered pillars spin a web of stone from the floor to the apex of the roof. From the north wall of the nave the minstrels' gallery projects, resting on niches; below them are carved heads representing Edward III and Queen Philippa. It was Edward who gave the Duchy of Cornwall to his eldest son, the city of Exeter included at a rent of £20 per year.

In the south transept a slab with three defaced figures marks the reputed burying place of Leofric; nearby is the imposing monument to Hugh Courtenay, Earl of Devon

1 **West Front**
2 **Nave**
3 Nave Pulpit
4 South Transept
 (St John's Tower)
5 Courtenay Tomb
6 Chapter House
7 Quire Screen
8 Quire
9 Lady Chapel
10 North Transept
 (St Paul's Tower)
11 North Porch
 (Minstrels' Gallery
 above)

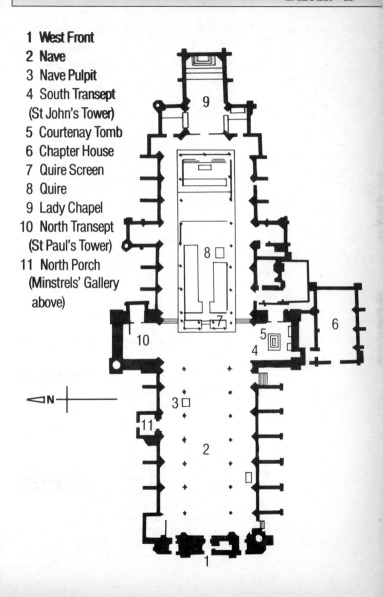

Rougemont House Museum of Costume and Lace

Rougemont House, Castle Street, Exeter, was originally built for Dr John Patch, an Exeter surgeon, in 1768, but was substantially altered in the early 19th century to its present elegant Regency style. Its gardens extend into the old moat of Exeter's castle, which, with its surviving Norman gateway, is Exeter's best kept secret.

A new Museum of Costume and Lace opened here in 1986 and it has rapidly become one of the most popular museums of its kind in the country. The costumes are beautifully displayed in appropriate period room settings where great trouble has been taken to ensure that the furnishings, pictures and ornaments compliment the clothes; the museum conversion has been done sensitively so that the house retains its domestic scale and character.

Naturally the highlight of the permanent exhibitions is the display of Honiton lace; one room is devoted entirely to this subject and in addition there are extensive reserve collections that can be consulted.

(died 1377) and his wife Margaret. Elsewhere there are several other memorials to bishops and one, by the west door, to R D Blackmore, the author of *Lorna Doone*.

The chapter house, off the south transept, is superb, the principal window a kaleidoscope of medieval glass fragments.

In the Quire, the bishop's throne is an incredible extravaganza of wood carving – fifty-two feet high – and constructed, apparently, without a single nail; the stalls are more modest, the misericords, dating from the thirteenth century, decorated with curious figures, including a mermaid, elephant and female centaur.

Outside the Cathedral, the Bishop's Palace is more or less hidden from view at the south-east corner of the great church. The green and Close encircle the north side, a popular meeting place for youngsters and convenient spot for office workers' lunches in the summer; the buildings display an array of styles from medieval to modern. There are ancient arched doorways revealing glimpses of private courtyard gardens and secluded corners of rough red stone adorned with wistaria and ivy. Sixteenth-century Mol's Coffee House, unfortunately no longer serving coffee, is one of the finest jettied and timber-framed houses in the city; next door, squeezed in the corner, is St Martin's, one of several small red sandstone churches in the city. The Royal Clarence Hotel claims to have been the first establishment in England to have assumed the French title of 'hotel'.

Through Martin's Lane, where the Old Ship Inn was frequented by Sir Francis Drake, to the High Street; turn left and on the opposite side the great stone portico forms the entrance to the Guildhall – the hall was built in 1330 making it one of the oldest municipal buildings still in regular use. The arched and braced roof timbers rest on carved bosses of bears holding staves, civic silver fills a cabinet in the gallery and the walls are hung with portraits of Exeter worthies. At the back are the old cells. Beyond the Guildhall a shopping precinct surrounds and dwarfs St Pancras Church; over a covered footbridge the Harlequin Centre provides additional prime trading sites.

Cross Queen Street to the Royal Albert Memorial Museum. Next door is the Devon and Exeter Arts Centre with a busy programme of temporary exhibitions and events. It is one of the venues for the increasingly successful Exeter Arts Festival, held in May and June. Cobbled Gandy Street, packed with wine bars and fashionable hairdressers, leads into Musgrave Row; turn left to Library Place. Take the steps or ramp up to the main entrance and on to Castle Street – Rougemont House on the left-hand side was opened in 1986 as a museum of costume and lace. The house was originally built for Dr John Patch, an Exeter surgeon, in 1768 but was substantially altered in the early 19th century to its present elegant Regency style. The costumes displayed date from the 1740s and are cleverly shown in appropriate room settings. One room is devoted entirely to Honiton lace.

Outside, the gardens are set in the moat of Rougemont Castle; the remains of the Norman gateway are impressive. Footpaths through Northernhay Gardens provide a good opportunity to appreciate the strategic value of the castle's site; the city walls, remarkably intact, mark the boundary of the Roman town, and much of the masonry is Roman.

Return to the High Street and cross to the Princesshay pedestrian precinct and the Underground Passages – the entrance resembles that of the nearby public lavatories – but here visitors are welcomed by a guide and can explore a rat-run of rock-cut and stone-built caverns, the medieval aqueducts that brought water to the city from wells beyond

Royal Albert Memorial Museum

On Queen Street in Exeter stands the imposing Victorian edifice that almost shouts 'museum', with its steep steps leading up from the pavement into the gaudily painted hall, recently restored to its original colour scheme. This is the flagship of Devon's museums and the one that, if any, could claim to hold a county collection; unfortunately much of the local material remains in store. The archaeology gallery offers a good introduction to the prehistory of Devon until the Roman period; there are displays of Devon pottery, Exeter silver, glassware and fine art – including some modern topographical work. There is also a Devonshire natural history gallery.

Much of the rest of the museum contains a medley of exotica: it is a standing joke that the moth-eaten giraffe will never be moved as the building must have been put up around him; there are elephants, crocodiles and kangaroos; American bison and Arctic seal; fabulous African wood carvings and of course an Egyptian mummy. One section has been preserved as a Victorian study collection of shells and corals; an Aladdin's cave of underwater life encased in heavy stained mahogany. The temporary exhibition gallery shows a lively variety of modern touring exhibitions, mainly artwork.

Exeter Maritime Museum
Strollers ambling along the east bank of the quay down by Exeter's historic custom-house may be surprised to find the brightly-painted prows of Portuguese fishing boats staring out at them from the cavernous warehouses that line the old river bank. Exeter Maritime Museum's international collection of ships and boats of every possible size and shape appears to be bulging out of every crevice.

A highlight for visitors must be the crossing of the river on the hand-hauled ferry, but this is not the only experience of seamanship; visitors are positively encouraged to climb aboard the Bahrain pearling *dhow*, the steam tug *Canute*, and *Bertha*, Brunel's dredger from Bridgwater (Somerset). There are primitive canoes from Papua New Guinea and Africa, a Venetian gondola, and the *Cygnet*, a rowing boat built with a swan's head figurehead.

One room exhibits the boats or wrecks that have survived the hair-brained adventures of Atlantic rowers; *Britannia* is here, the vessel in which John Fairfax completed the first successful single-handed rowing of the Atlantic; but so too is the *Puffin* in which David Johnstone and John Hoare met their deaths in 1966.

The museum aims to rescue boats going out of use from all over the world; it claims this is one of the largest international collections.

the walls. At this east end of the High Street most of whatever was left unscathed by the bombs of the Second World War has been redeveloped; across the junction with New North Road and Paris Street, the same story continues into Sidwell Street. Only Exeter has a street called Sidwell Street, named after the city's own saint who was martyred, beheaded with a scythe, near the corner of Well Street and York Road – a modern (1969) fibreglass sculpture by Frederick Irving on the wall of Tesco's supermarket depicts her. The ancient medieval church of St Sidwell's was rebuilt in 1812 to a neo-Gothic design; that church was destroyed in 1942; the present church was built in 1957–8. Over the roundabout at the junction of Old Tiverton Road and Blackboy Road, St Ann's Chapel and 16th-century almshouses enclose a delightful courtyard; the chapel is on loan to the Greek Orthodox community.

At the opposite end of the High Street, the road drops away steeply down Fore Street to the river; a narrow path to the right leads to St Nicholas Priory – one of the most fascinating and important buildings in the city, but little visited. The Benedictine Priory was founded in 1070 by monks from Battle Abbey, Sussex. Surviving features include the Norman undercroft, a splendid 15th-century guest hall and kitchen and fine plaster ceilings. Back on Fore Street, cross into Market Street: turn right into Smythen Street which narrows into Stepcote Hill, the medieval main road into the city from the west. At the bottom, St Mary Steps is another surviving city church; it possesses a Norman font and a fine wooden screen. The famous clock was intended to represent Henry VIII and two javelin men, but is known locally as Matthew the Miller and his two sons. Opposite, a plaque on the old wall marks the site of the Westgate. The timber-framed Tudor building is 'The House that Moved'; in 1961 it was in the way of a new road, so was strapped and jacked and rolled to its present site to preserve it for posterity.

Cross the main road to the traffic island, encircled by ring road and bridges, and here, strangely marooned from the rest of the city, lie the remains of the medieval bridge over the Exe; cross again into Commercial Road and follow this down to the quay. Hugely improved by recent restoration schemes, the quay area has become a focus for leisure interests and activities; the historic setting formed a natural backdrop for the filming of some scenes in *The Onedin Line*. Sturdy warehouses have now been converted to stylish restaurants and discotheques. Beside the custom-house, built in 1681, and guarded by two cannon, the new interpretation centre in the Quay House is a good place to start a tour; there is a small exhibition illustrating the goods that were once imported from here and children can take away a souvenir print from one of the blocks that were used to stamp bales of woollen cloth; upstairs there is an excellent audio-visual programme.

Exeter Maritime Museum

The canal basin is a hive of industry with the Exeter Maritime Museum and boating enthusiasts permanently rubbing and scrubbing their craft; there are river- and canal-side walks, fringed by reeds and meadows, to Countess Wear, with the Double Locks Inn about two miles downstream from the Quay.

TOPSHAM

South-east Devon can be conveniently explored from Exeter, or holiday-makers may prefer to stay in one of the seaside towns and use that as the hub of their tours. The following itinerary follows the eastern shore of the Exe estuary to Exmouth. As a pleasurable alternative to road travel, a branch line from Exeter Central Station heads for Exmouth via Topsham, Exton and Lympstone.

From Exeter, South Street leads out of the

city to Countess Wear; the road passes under the M5 and immediately enters **Topsham**, an ancient and fascinating port situated where the river broadens into the estuary. There was a Roman port here from the middle of the first century, then a Saxon settlement, the property of the monastery of St Mary and St Peter in Exeter. In 1282 the Countess of Devon built a weir across the river Exe (hence Countess Wear), cutting Exeter off from the sea and thus ensuring that all merchandise for the city had to be unloaded at Topsham – to the benefit of the Countess's coffers.

The canal to Exeter, avoiding the weir, was not built until the second half of the 16th century, and even then Topsham continued to dominate as an outport of the city. There was considerable trade in woollen serges with Holland, and returning vessels brought back Dutch bricks as ballast and Dutch architectural styles.

As the main road enters the town there are a number of narrow lanes to the right – down to the riverside; the rest of the tour of the town should be made on foot.

The road leading downstream is known as The Strand; facing the estuary and with magnificent views across the water and marshes to wooded hills are a number of Dutch-gabled houses. Many use their first floors, with the view, as the living area, leaving the ground floor for garaging and, as often as not, winter boat-storage. One house on the Strand, Follett Lodge, a peculiar mix of styles overlain with pink render, was the home of Sir William Webb Follett (1798-1845), the Attorney General; in Lord Hatherley's estimation 'in every qualification of intellect and grace of manner he was as nearly perfect as man can be.'

Just beyond is the Passage House Inn, a low-slung pub packed with character and beams; in front of it the old ferry still plies to and fro across the river: a notice gives prices for people, prams, dogs and cycles.

The shipbuilding yards are now mostly unused, and the ancient stone warehouses store laid-up pleasure yachts; but the estuary buzzes with outboard motors and the rigging of the moored boats twangs in the wind.

Further on down the Strand is Topsham Museum, founded by Dorothy Holman, who built up the collection and lived in the house, now the museum, for 45 years. It is a charming place with a sun-trap courtyard garden where visitors can enjoy teas of home-made cakes and Devonshire cream. The museum illustrates the long history of Topsham, particularly the importance of the port; there is a superb model of the town as it was in 1900. Several rooms have been recreated as 18th-century period settings – the parlour is very effective. Notice Tom Putt's coat and waistcoat; it was he who developed the Tom Putt apple in his orchards at Combe House, Gittisham.

The little town is pleasing, too: the main road curves off over the railway line towards Lympstone and Exmouth, leaving the narrow High Street untroubled by through traffic. The Salutation, a particularly fine 18th-century inn, has a pillared porch over the pavement; the other pubs have a nautical flavour – the Steam Packet Inn, Lord Nelson, Lighter Inn and the Globe. There are several high quality restaurants, a number of antique shops and a very traditional-looking grocers, W A Nott, beside the cobbled path leading to the church.

From Topsham take the A376 towards Exmouth. **Lympstone** is dominated on the main road by the Royal Marines training camp, but it is worth a short detour to the tiny harbour on the estuary, where wooden ships were once built and launched. There is a pleasant mixture of thatched cottages and early Georgian houses. After the first town sign for Exmouth, turn left down a country lane to

A-la-Ronde

Exmouth

Population: 28,661

Early Closing: Wed

Cashpoints: *Barclays* 12 Rolle St; *Lloyds* 22 The Strand; *Midland* 1 Rolle St; *NatWest* 11 Rolle St

Tourist Information: Alexandra Terrace (summer only)

Attractions: A La Ronde*, Country Life Museum*

Arts: Exmouth Players, Blackmore Theatre

Cinema: The Savoy

By Road: London 173 miles (A376, M5, M4), Exeter 11 miles (A376)

By Rail: ½hr to Exeter plus 2hrs 15mins from Exeter to London (London, Paddington to Penzance line). Connections to Barnstaple and Newton Abbot via Exeter.

A-la-Ronde, a fairytale thatched house, built in 1795 by Jane and Mary Parminter. It is not in fact round, but 16-sided, containing 20 rooms around a central octagon, 45ft high and modelled on a Byzantine basilica; a gallery is decorated with shells.

Exmouth is a traditional seaside resort, with two miles of golden sands; the town stands at the mouth of the Exe estuary, where the sea sweeps in round Straight Point. Half-submerged sands stretch from Dawlish Warren, on the west side of the estuary, leaving a narrow channel to be negotiated by vessels heading up-stream to Topsham and Exeter and similarly narrow access to Exmouth's busy port.

The estuary, sheltered by the Warren, is dotted with pleasure craft and freckled with sails in the summer, with the blue-grey hills of Haldon rising behind. The sunsets are superb, and even fired the genius of Turner. Past the railway station and towards the docks, on the estuary side of the town, red brick cottages line the streets, backing onto the beach, littered with small craft and, at low tide, picked by waders and gulls. Shelly Road prefabs form a shanty town of holiday homes; sandy slips between the bungalows lead down to the shore where crab pots and nets are mended against a backdrop of boulders and the sea wall.

Towering cranes, capacious warehouses, oily quays and dockland pubs surround the dock basin where cargo vessels enter and leave through a narrow channel, like a short stretch of high-walled canal. After loading their cargo at the quayside, the mooring ropes are unhitched and a local pilot, assisted by two tug boats, gingerly edges the huge boats through; the tugs nudge the boats gently into position before they squeeze past the swing footbridge and out to sea.

Cross over the swing bridge and pass the custom-house and fresh fish shop to the

Esplanade – Exmouth's sea front. The clock tower was a gift to the town from the Lord of the Manor, the Hon. Mark Rolle, on the occasion of Queen Victoria's Diamond Jubilee. Sea and river trips are offered from the beach and there are children's rides and various refreshment kiosks – the sands stretch for a couple of miles towards Orcombe Point, a rocky headland. Opposite the Maer, a pleasant open green sward, Maer Rocks provide a low-water playground of rock pools, scuttling crabs and seaweed. The Esplanade becomes Marine Drive and then Queen's Drive as it nears the Point; here footpaths lead up over the cliffs to Sandy Bay and beyond.

Back towards the town, above the Esplanade, a fine terrace of Georgian town houses, at the Beacon, illustrates the popularity of Exmouth in the 18th century; Lady Nelson stayed at number 6, and Lady Byron at number 19. The town was also acclaimed as a health centre, ideal for 'weakly children and those of a scrofulous constitution'.

AXMINSTER

Close to the Dorset border and still on a busy transport route, **Axminster** was originally sited at the intersection of two Roman roads, the Fosseway and Icknield Street, although archaeological remains from the neighbourhood suggest an even earlier foundation. The hub of the town is the parish church of St Mary the Virgin; tradition recalls that the body of Cynehard the Atheling was brought here for burial in AD 786, and that King Athelstan endowed the church in AD 937. No clear evidence of a Saxon church survives, but there is a Norman doorway opening onto the east end of the south aisle. Beneath a carved arch in the chancel lies the effigy of Alicia (she died in 1287), the wife of Reginald de Mohun, the founder of a Cistercian abbey about a mile from the town down by the

King Athelstan

One of the most important battles in early British history occurred just outside Axminster in 937, when King Athelstan defeated marauding invaders from Scotland and the North at the Battle of Brunanburgh. The grandson of King Alfred, Athelstan fostered the dream of a united kingdom and even before he became king he defeated the Welsh and Danes to bring stability to much of the country.

He was crowned in 925 at the age of thirty and rather than continue the wars he allowed the outlying regions to keep their rulers if they paid allegiance to him. A tribute to his success was the fact that for the first time a common coinage was introduced, bearing his head and the words 'King of all Britain'.

The battle at Brunanburgh finally established the truth of these words. He endowed Axminster church with seven priests – the number of Earls who had died in the battle.

Athelstan not only stabilised his own kingdom but made many links to Europe, mostly through marriage; he gave one sister in marriage to Otto, Holy Roman Emperor, the most powerful ruler on the continent, and another to Hugh the Great whose line produced the kings of France until 1848. Athelstan died in 940 having created the boundaries of Britain which we know today.

Honiton Lace
The town of Honiton has been associated with lace-making since the 16th century, when religious persecution in Holland sent craftsmen to Devon, where they taught the local people their skills. Although called Honiton Lace many villages nearby were involved in the production: Colaton Raleigh, Branscombe, Beer and even some parts of Somerset and Dorset. However by its situation on the main route between London and the West Country, Honiton became the natural marketing centre.

Also known as 'Pillow Lace', because it is worked on a pillow or cushion held on the knees, or 'Bone Lace', the bobbins being made from sheep's trotters, the industry thrived until the late 17th century, when mechanisation led to a cheaper product, but the worst blow came when a lace factory was opened in Tiverton in 1815.

An order for Queen Victoria's wedding dress was given to Jane Bidney of Beer, the work being shared by 100 workers, and this revitalised the industry and created the demand for individualised orders that is the mainstay of the present-day lace-makers and cannot be superseded by machines. The Royal Family continue to have a close link: the Princess Royal, Princess Alice and the present Princess of Wales have all had lace from Honiton to decorate their wedding dresses.

river; only fragments of the walls remain at Higher Newenham Farm. The other effigy is of the first vicar of Axminster, Gervase de Prestaller.

Also in the church is a small sample of one of Axminster's most famous products – a bit of carpet; this piece was from one of the first carpets made by Thomas Whitty, the inventor, in 1755, of the Axminster method. Whitty's process was apparently so painstaking and laborious that when a carpet was completed the church bells were rung, carriages came from far and wide and the carpet was carried in procession from the old factory to the church for blessing before despatch. Carpet-making prospered until 1835 when manufacturing ceased; it has recently been revived and visitors are welcomed at the new carpet factory in Woodmead Road, just past the railway station.

South of the church, in Church Street, Axminster Museum occupies part of the former 19th-century Court House and Police Station; the museum illustrates the history of the town and includes archaeology, relics of the Civil War and the christening gloves worn by John Churchill, the first Duke of Marlborough, when he was christened in the chapel of nearby Ashe House.

On the other side of the church, where the Chard and Bridport roads meet, stands the George Hotel, a magnificent Georgian coaching inn; the origins of the building go back to the 16th century and Oliver Cromwell is reputed to have stayed here. Above the archway is the Adam Room, with a magnificent fireplace, minstrels' gallery and Venetian windows. George III ate in this room on the occasion of his visit to Axminster Carpets in 1789.

From Axminster the A35 winds through valleys of rich pasture to **Honiton**; as the road descends steeply into the town notice the castellated toll house, the Copper Castle, on

the left and the surviving toll gate. Through
traffic from the A35 and A30 trunk road now
bypasses the town to the north, so the two-
mile long main street, though busy, is at least
spared the thunder of monstrous juggernauts.
Ironically it was this traffic and the hustle of
merchants and travellers that originally
brought prosperity to the town. The A30
follows, more or less, the line of the Roman
road to Exeter and near this important junction
with the road from Dorchester a settlement
developed.

The first site was on the hill south of the
town where St Michael's Church still stands;
then, in about 1200, William de Redvers
founded a new town right beside the main
road; New Street links the old with the new.
For generations, church-going was a problem
for the elderly and infirm, who had to stagger
up the hill to the old church, until 1835 when
St Paul's was built in the centre of the town on
the north side of the High Street.

Beside St Paul's, Allhallows Museum,
housed in a chapel of c1200, contains a wealth
of local history depicting Honiton's various
claims to fame: cloth-manufacturing, lace and
pottery. This was the first of the great serge-
manufacturing towns in Devon and there was
a flourishing woollen industry in the 17th and
18th centuries. Lace-making was introduced by
Flemish refugees in the reign of Elizabeth I; the
earliest record of 'bonelace' can be found on
the tomb of James Rodge in St Michael's
churchyard. The Honiton Lace Shop, where
examples of modern and antique lace can be
purchased, together with bobbins, cottons and
do-it-yourself manuals, is towards the east end
of the High Street on the south side. Several
fine Georgian coaching inns once competed for
business on either side of the road; the stables
and tackrooms of the Dolphin and Black Lion
have been converted to pedestrian shopping
precincts; in 'Dolphin Court' a hand-written

Making lace

sign recalls the days when coaches thundered in and all hands set to, changing the horses, feeding the passengers and passing on the gossip: 'Marker, Ostler, Post boy'.

The town is set on the south bank of the River Otter, named apparently for the multitude of otters that were once to be found; this is the countryside Defoe described as 'the most beautiful landskip in the world, a mere picture.'

The A30 follows the Roman road from Honiton towards Exeter; 4 miles from Honiton turn left down the B3177, signposted to **Ottery St Mary**. The road enters this delightful country town through a street of pleasant Georgian town houses opening to a vista of the magnificent twin-towered church of St Mary – the pride of Ottery and the finest parish church in Devon. In 1337 John de Grandisson, Bishop of Exeter, purchased the manor of Ottery back from Rouen in order to create a College of Canons here; between 1337 and 1342 he enlarged the original church, modelling it closely on the great Cathedral Church of St Peter in Exeter. The church interior, though defaced at the dissolution, is superb: the richly coloured and carved roof bosses are a particular feature; note also the 14th-century altar screen, the Lady Chapel and the steadily ticking medieval clock in the south transept. The canopied tombs of Sir Otto and Lady Beatrix de Grandisson, who died in 1359 and 1374 respectively, are impressive. The College, 'a sanctuary for piety and learning', consisted of 40 members including eight choristers and a master of grammar. South of the church in the lane known as 'The College', several of the old school buildings survive, mostly dating from the 16th century.

After the dissolution the school was refounded as 'The King's New Grammar School'. In the mid-18th century the Rev. John Coleridge was appointed Master, later also

St Mary's, Ottery St Mary

becoming vicar; he produced 13 children by two wives, the youngest being Samuel Taylor (1772–1834), the poet and philosopher. The bronze plaque in the churchyard wall, with his profile and looming albatross, commemorates Samuel's childhood in the town – recalled in his poem 'Songs of the Pixies':

. . . Then with quaint music hymn the parting
  gleam
By lonely Otter's sleep persuading dream.

The weathercock on the tower is reputed to be the oldest *in situ* in Europe: for over 500 years it emitted a siren-like noise from cleverly tuned tubes inserted in the breast of the cock by medieval craftsmen; however, a 20th-century clean-up resulted in a ghastly howl from even the slightest gust and the tubes were blocked.

From the Market Place below the church, Gold Street and Silver Street meet at a narrow junction marked by a neat bank, a knob on the apex of its roof. The narrows continue until Broad Street, the principal shopping thoroughfare. The town suffered a disastrous fire in 1866, so many of the buildings are Victorian, but some fine Georgian houses survive, notably the Priory in Paternoster Row. From Broad Street the streets fan out – the names are charming: Yonder Street, Longdods Lane, Tip Hill, Amen Court and Jesu Street. Down Mill Street, behind the Otter Mill, is a unique 'tumbling weir' – a circular hole in the mill leat down which the water tumbles to drive the mill machinery. It was built in 1790. Ottery was a woollen-manufacturing centre and an important market for local produce; Daniel Defoe recounts that in the 1720s '20,000 hogsheads of cider [were sent] hence every year to London, and which is still worse, that it is most of it bought there by the merchants to mix with their wines.'

About a mile south of the town Knightstone

Ottery Tar Barrels
Flaming tar barrels in Ottery St Mary on 5th November provide an awesome spectacle, which, with the accompanying carnival, fair and firework festivities attract huge crowds. The custom dates from the end of the 18th century, and despite numerous attempts to ban it on safety grounds, it continues to flourish.

Early anti-papist feelings are held partly responsible for the zeal and fervour of such celebrations in Devonshire. The religious implications of Guy Fawkes' plot to blow up the Houses of Parliament were essentially to create access for a new government to restore the country to Roman Catholicism. This drew strong outbursts from Protestant strongholds, especially in the towns which had suffered the heresy burnings under Catholic Queen Mary. With the excuse for jollification at the failure of the 'gunpowder plot', many customs were established around the occasion, and the tar barrels of Ottery are a splendid example.

After the huge bonfire has been lit in St Saviour's Meadows, and the Guy is well-licked by the flames, participants, with faces greased to avoid scorching, and wearing thick protective clothes, swing the burning tar barrels onto their shoulders and race, in a seemingly haphazard manner down the High Street.

Sir Walter Raleigh
Born at Hayes Barton, near Budleigh Salterton, in 1552, Walter Raleigh's childhood dream of the sea was captured in the famous painting by Sir John Everett Millais 'The Boyhood of Raleigh', showing the young boy listening spellbound to the yarns of a fisherman.

As a young, brave and outstandingly handsome adventurer Raleigh made his reputation as a successful sailor and explorer.

Raleigh is remembered particularly for his role in introducing tobacco and the potato to Britain, both from the Americas; he himself never actually went to America, but he did use his wealth to finance a number of voyages and an early colony.

His relationship with and marriage to Elizabeth Throgmorton removed him from favour with the Queen and he was imprisoned in the Tower for treason. On the accession of James I he was tried and again imprisoned, on this occasion in the Bloody Tower; he lived in a suite of rooms in some comfort with his wife and family for sixteen years. He was released in order that he should organise an exploratory voyage to South America, with strict instructions that on no account should he attack the Spanish. Unfortunately while he was lying below decks sick with fever, one of his subordinates attacked a Spanish garrison; back home he was imprisoned again until his execution on 29 October 1618.

Manor is one of the most complete examples of a fourteenth century manor house in the country; it is not, unfortunately, open to the public. Cadhay House, a mile north-west of Ottery, over Cadhay Bridge, is open and is well worth a visit: it is a mixture of Tudor and Georgian design around a courtyard.

BUDLEIGH SALTERTON AND THE SOUTH-EAST COAST
Budleigh Salterton is a quiet and rather select seaside spot, largely on account of its stony beach. The bay stretches from **Straight Point** to **Otterton Ledge**, a distance of more than two miles. Bathing here is strictly for strong swimmers: the shore shelves steeply from a coarse ridge of fat round pebbles, 'like buns or muffins'. The same pebbles decorate garden walls and garden paths around the town, and are collected by visitors to adorn their windowsills or use as paperweights.

The main road drops from Knowle down to the sea front, one long street known variously as West Hill, High Street, Fore Street, South Parade, and Marine Parade along the sea front; beside the road, for much of the distance, flows a small stream, with little stone-slab bridges across to give access to the houses and shops.

It is a pretty and unhurried place, with abundant tearooms and tempting window displays of home-baked scones and crusty Devon cream. Budleigh became popular, in a genteel way, during the Napoleonic Wars and grew rapidly after the peace of 1815; its late Georgian and Regency houses and cottages are particularly elegant, and look fresh and well cared for. Sir John Everett Millais lived for a time at 'The Octagon', at the west end of the Parade, and painted his well-known picture *The Boyhood of Raleigh* there; it was exhibited at the Royal Academy in 1870. Raleigh was born a couple of miles away at East Budleigh.

Opposite Mackerel Square, where it is easy to imagine the fishermen laying out their catch for sale to the local housewives, stands the Fairlynch Museum and Arts Centre, an odd thatched building with a little thatched dome on its roof. Inside it is charming; displays illustrate the history of the town, including the smugglers' cellar, and there are regular exhibitions of local artists' work.

On the beach, winches haul the fishing boats up on to the shingle ridge, beyond the reach of the tide; fishing tackle, nets and crab and lobster pots mingle with the intriguing sea-washed debris of winter storms. Beach huts, in pastel shades, provide changing rooms and convenient shelter from the sea breezes. Beyond the town on each side, steep red sandstone cliffs rise up to 300ft, with glorious cliff-top walks.

On the east side of the Otter valley **Otterton** is a picturesque village of cob cottages and chestnut trees. The old mill beside the river has been converted into an interesting working museum; two water wheels, made by Bodley Bros of Exeter, power the three-storey mill, grinding wholewheat flour; bread, cakes and savoury pies are made on the premises. Other exhibitions include Honiton lace and a gallery of fine art and craft.

About a mile from Otterton, **Ladram Bay** forms a sheltered east-facing cove; the caravan park and restaurant are hidden from the beach which is pebbly but good for swimming. From the bay, the South Devon Coast Path rises north and south to the cliff tops. The route to Sidmouth scales High Peak, then drops down Windgate to the town, a distance of about 3 miles.

A minor road from Otterton follows the valley of a short tributary of the river Otter, before descending Peak Hill into **Sidmouth**.

On Christmas Eve 1819, the Duke and Duchess of Kent arrived in Sidmouth with

Bicton Park
Fourteen miles south-east of Exeter and just inland from Budleigh Salterton, Bicton Park offers a family day out with a variety of features. There are 50 acres of gardens which blaze with seasonal colour – shrubs, woodlands, lakes, ponds and fountains. The Italian Garden was commissioned in 1734 by Sir Henry Rolle and attributed to Andre le Notre, the designer of the gardens at the Palace of Versailles. The Palm House is magnificent, with tropical and sub-tropical sections – bananas even ripen here. Specialist interests are catered for in the Fuchsia and Geranium houses and the recently opened Orchid House.

A modern building houses the James Countryside Museum, an interesting collection of agricultural tools and equipment, with horse-drawn waggons, ancient tractors and a superb wooden-screw cider press. There are numerous working models, a brass-rubbing centre and an exhibition of breadmaking through the ages.

Nearby an open-air arena is used regularly for all manner of equestrian events and other activities which bring the site to life; a recent annual innovation is the Bicton Clowns' Day, when as many as 30 clowns from all over the country assemble here for a hilarious jamboree.

The Ashen Faggot
A Devon variation of the traditional Yule Log, the Ashen Faggot consisted of a bunch of ash twigs and small branches, bound together by withies and ceremoniously brought into the house on Christmas Eve. The large open fireplaces of the Devon farmhouses enabled the faggot to be as long as seven feet and weigh up to a hundredweight. Ash was used because it was said that Mary and Joseph lit a fire of ash to warm the stable at the first Christmas; a more mundane explanation is that it is wood that burns well while still green and the branches were meant to be cut as near to Christmas as possible.

Although ash was reputed to have many magical properties, the more down-to-earth festivities of the occasion seem to have dominated: as the faggot burned the withies snapped with loud reports – heralding the call for another round of cider for all those present. Sometimes the faggot was used for divination: the unmarried members of the party would each choose a withy, and whoever's snapped first was going to be the first to be married in the following year.

their daughter, the Princess Victoria, to seek seclusion from the Duke's creditors. They were suffering from what he himself described as 'gilded poverty' and where better to retreat than this quiet seaside hamlet? The Kents stayed at Woolbrook Cottage, now known as the Royal Glen. The Duke died here in 1820 and the family returned to London. Victoria never visited Sidmouth again, but in 1866 she presented a stained-glass window to the parish church in memory of her father.

Although Sidmouth has grown considerably since those days, it has retained much of its Regency style as well as a pleasant air of tranquil gentility. The mile-long Esplanade is backed by York Terrace, a stately row of balconied Georgian houses with ironwork railings and sparkling brass door knobs. Beach House, also on the Esplanade, is a perfect example of sea-front architecture of that period, painted strawberry pink and white, with coloured glass in leaded panes and a decorative balcony over the bay window.

From the 1780s Sidmouth was increasingly patronised by the wealthy, who built ornate cottages in every sheltered spot with views over the bay; many have since been converted into hotels. As the town grew in popularity, terraces of lodging houses were built, like Clifton Place and Elysian Fields; Fortfield Terrace, a shallow crescent with first-floor balconies, looks out over the bowling green towards the sea.

Sidmouth grew up as a little fishing village, described in the 17th century as 'one of the especialist fisher towns of the shire'; the boats in winter were hauled up the shingle beach to protect them from storms. The town is sheltered by tremendous red sandstone cliffs that rise on both sides to over 500ft at Peak Hill and Salcombe Hill, west and east respectively. John Betjeman enthused: 'If it were not for the sea, Sidmouth, I thought, would be tropic forest. Devon hills protect it on all but the seaward side . . . Huge cliffs, shaved down almost sheer, stretch pinkly to the east until they change to the white chalk of the Dorset coast.'

Opposite the parish church of St Giles and St Nicholas, patron saint of sailors, Sidmouth Museum portrays the Victorian resort: note the gruesome barber-surgeon's signboard and the poor albatross's swollen foot, used as a tobacco pouch; the museum has an interesting collection of local prints, a costume gallery and a good display of exquisite lace. A plaque on the wall of the neighbouring cottage records that Stephen Reynolds, 1881–1919, 'Fisherman's Friend, social reformer and author worked here.'

For more than 30 years Sidmouth has played host to the remarkable International Festival of Folk Arts, usually held in early August: it has become a cosmopolitan extravaganza of music and dancing tradition from all over the world. The Grand Finale of the occasion is the torchlight procession through the streets of the town.

From Sidmouth the A3052 follows an inland route to **Seaton**; the villages of **Branscombe** and **Beer** are worth a detour.

Sidmouth

Branscombe is a scattered village of pretty stone and thatch cottages that snuggle in the three deep combes of the tributaries of the little stream that flows out through the shingle at Branscombe Mouth. The valleys are verdant and tree-lined and sheltered on all sides with only a narrow opening to the sea. Eastwards the chalk cliffs rise to over 400ft, westwards to over 500ft. At **Hooken Cliff**, between Branscombe and Beer Head, a dramatic landslip occurred in 1790 when 10 acres of land dropped 200ft towards the sea, creating a wilderness of columns and pinnacles now tangled in undergrowth.

There is no village centre, but the ancient

Sidmouth

Population: 11,434

Early Closing: Thu

Cashpoints: *Lloyds* High St; *Midland* Fore St; *NatWest* 52 High St

Tourist Information: Esplanade (summer only)

Attractions: Sidmouth Museum*, Vintage Toy and Train Museum*

Leisure: Manor Pavilion

By Road: London 164 miles (A375, A303, M3), Exeter 15 miles (B3175, A3052), Honiton 15 miles (A375)

By Rail: Nearest main-line station is at Honiton (3hrs from London on the Waterloo to Exeter line).

church of St Winifred, perched on the hillside of the westernmost combe, has been a focus of life for at least 800 years. The church once belonged to Benedictine monks from Exeter; the central castle-like tower and nave are Norman. There is a most unusual 18th-century three-decker pulpit, and a few fragments of a medieval wall painting, probably representing Belshazzar's Feast. In the churchyard is the tomb of John Hurley, a customs officer, who died in 1755: he was endeavouring to put out a fire on the cliffs, lit as a signal to smugglers, when he missed his footing and fell to his death.

At the bottom of the hill, by the modern village hall, the National Trust has preserved the old village smithy; far from being a fossilized museum-piece, though, the smithy continues to offer a service and the lady-smith is a farrier to boot.

The last of the chain of houses and cottages, nearest the sea, is Great Seaside Farm, also owned by the National Trust; unfortunately it is not open to the public, but from the road it presents a traditional picture of idyllic rural England, with hens scratching in the yard surrounded by mellow stone farm buildings and the Elizabethan farmhouse under a neatly thatched roof. From here a track leads down to the beach-side car-park.

The village of **Beer**, only a mile from Seaton, is protected from the westerly winds by the embracing arm of Beer Head's high white chalk cliffs; the shingle beach faces east. A fishing fleet of half a dozen boats is based here; their tackle litters the shore above the high tide mark and their catch is sold direct from a tiny fish shop tucked under the cliff.

Beer was long known as a haunt of smugglers; one of the most notable, Jack Rattenbury, was a native of the village and operated from here. He had to give up his career in his fifties when gout got the better of him, and in 1837 he published an account of his adventures, *Memoirs of a Smuggler*.

The main street is flanked by cottages and shops in cob and thatch and the famous Beer stone; beside the pavement a stream runs down a culvert to the sea; on the higher valley sides detached villas look out to the broad horizon. Beer stone has been quarried since Roman times; in Devon it is particularly regarded for its use in Exeter cathedral. Part of the quarry, about a mile west of the village, is now open to the public. Here cavernous underground chambers, their walls marked by ancient tools, are supported by great square pillars of stone, like subterranean cathedrals in themselves.

The B3174 continues into **Seaton**, Devon's easternmost seaside resort, just 152 miles from London; it lies on the west side of the mouth of the river Axe. The original village was around the church, about half a mile inland beside the estuarine mudflats and pasture.

A port of some significance developed at the mouth of the estuary when the River Axe more or less filled the valley, but by the 16th century a bar of stones and pebbles had built up, narrowing the river to the channel on the east side of the valley. The 16th-century writer John Leland described the fruitless efforts of the 'Men of Seton' to divert the course of the Axe: they tried to dig away the pebble ridge in order to re-establish their safe harbour for trading and fishing vessels. By the 17th century it was realised that further work was useless, so a bank was built beside the marshes on the estuary to reclaim the ground and create fresh pasture land; that bank was later used for a branch railway and now the Seaton trams, a popular visitor attraction, run along it for a couple of miles before crossing the river and rising to terminus at Colyton.

The beach, off the ridge, slopes steadily and steeply into the sea; a wonderful south-facing

Seaton tram

crescent backed by tall cliffs of red stone on one side and white chalk on the other. The little town and esplanade were late to develop, but the gardens and parks make up for any lack of monuments or impressive buildings. Windsor Garden, in front of the Town Hall, specialises in roses; in the spring and summer the Jubilee gardens around the brick clock tower on the west side of town are awash with colour.

Behind the beach road, a secondary road passes the Tram Station before crossing the River Axe; a mile upstream lies the little village of **Axmouth**. In the 16th century, according to John Leland, 'Seton towne (was) but a meane thing' and Axmouth 'an olde and bigge Fischer towne'; certainly in Roman times the largest ships could navigate safely up the river on the flood-tide to moor at Axmouth.

Today the little village is quiet and pretty, with colour-washed cottages under thatched roofs; the Old Harbour Inn, opposite the church, is reputed to be one of the oldest surviving buildings. The church is particularly interesting with substantial remains of Norman work, some medieval frescos and the tomb of the vicar, Roger Hariel, who died in 1324; the sparkling flint tower at the west end provided a vantage point over the harbour and estuary.

The area is a haven for birds: winter migrants find shelter and food on the river banks; redshank, shell duck, wigeon, teal, oyster catcher and capwing are regularly spotted, herons breed locally and kingfishers are commonly seen. On the sea cliffs about a mile south of Axmouth a great landslip occurred at Christmas 1839; a chasm ¾ mile long, 300ft wide, and 150ft deep formed when 8,000,000 tons of earth crashed in one night. The resulting jungle of foliage offers a rich habitat and is now a protected nature reserve.

CREDITON

Crediton takes its name from the River Creedy which flows near the town; it is a sheltered spot, in a shallow valley running east-west with the High Street on the south side. The blood-red rock and soil roundabout has coloured both the building stone and the local bricks; it is a fertile region once famed for its cider apples, but now mainly pastoral. The town and shops have a distinctly rural flavour and cater for a wide agricultural hinterland.

The principal blot on the town is the main road, the A377, from Exeter to Barnstaple, which mars the main street; luckily it is wide enough to cope with thundering lorries, but the planned by-pass will bring welcome relief. Off the main road, side streets reveal delightful cottages in cob and brick. The town suffered from disastrous fires in the 18th century, so few of the medieval buildings have survived; only in the quaint and narrow Dean Street, opposite the church, can examples of the old red sandstone cottages which survived the fires be seen.

Winfrith, better known as St Boniface, was born here c680 and is commemorated by a statue in the park; he became Abbot of Nursling, and with great fervour spread the Christian message through Europe. He was the first Christian preacher to visit Central Germany, where he founded the famous monastery of Fulda.

In the 10th century, a cathedral was built here with Eadulf as the first bishop; it was not until 1050 that the ecclesiastical headquarters were moved to Exeter, to be within the protection of the walled city. The grandeur of the present parish church, though much later in date, reflects Crediton's religious history; at the east end of the High Street, it is built in the local red sandstone, with a tower reminiscent of Exeter Cathedral.

From Crediton the A3072 twists and turns

St Boniface

In AD 680 a son was born to a minor British nobleman in the small town of Kirton, now Crediton, who was to become the patron saint of Germany and Holland. He was born Wynfrith, and later took the Latinized name Boniface. From an early age he showed a profound love of the church, entering the monastery in Exeter at 13. He quickly rose to prominence and was nominated to be the abbot in the monastery at Nutscelle near Winchester when only in his mid 30s; he avoided the appointment because he saw his role as a missionary, driven by what he described as 'the love of travel and the fear of Christ'.

In 718 he left England and for the next 35 years travelled through much of eastern Europe, particularly Germany, preaching and talking. He was a powerful speaker, using the forces of argument and reason, but on one occasion, infuriated by the resilience of pagan belief in the god Thor, he felled a sacred tree in full view of the worshippers, to demonstrate the superiority of his own faith.

Eventually his zeal led to his death. In 755 he set out on a journey to Friesland where at Dokkum he was set upon by a crowd of pagans and he and his 50 followers were slaughtered. His body was taken to the abbey at Fulda, where he was buried; he is still honoured as the 'Apostle of Germany'.

Killerton House
The Bear House, a strange 'organic' thatched hut, built from wood, with teeth as a floor, is one of the oddities to be found in the superb gardens of Killerton House, seven miles north of Exeter, near Broadclyst. Owned by the National Trust, it was the home of the Acland family, who had held the estate, one of the largest in Devon, since the Civil War. In the stables there is an exhibition on the family and its influence. The 18th-century house, built for the 7th Baronet and designed by John Johnson, contains the Paulise de Bush costume collection, a series of rooms each furnished in styles dating from the 18th century to the present day, and the gardens are a delight – formal herbaceous borders and wide lawns sweep down from the hillside to an open vista of parkland. In spring the wide range of magnolias and azaleas provide a colourful backdrop to the numerous varieties of trees, and Dolbury Hill behind the house, a landmark for miles around, affords splendid views of the Clyst and Culm valleys.

through the humpy and beautiful landscape of east Devon. Signposted to Thorverton, a short detour to **Cadbury Castle Hill Fort** and **Fursdon**, about 6 miles north-east of Crediton, is recommended.

Few English families can claim such a pedigree as the Fursdons of Fursdon House, Cadbury; records show that Walter de Fursdon was established in the manor of Cadbury before 1272. The house dates back to the 16th century, a stone fireplace, panelling and carvings surviving from this period; but the bulk of the present building is 18th century, the work of George Fursdon in the 1730s. The library and Ionic colonnade were added in 1815 and in 1818 respectively. From the gardens, best known for their Luccombe Oak, there are extensive views towards Exeter.

Back on the A3072 it is just two miles to **Bickleigh**, a picture-postcard village of white-washed cottages with thatched roofs deep in the valley of the River Exe. On either side of the 16th-century bridge the slopes rise to 700ft or so, steep and wooded, and in the valley bottom cattle graze the rich water meadows.

The river powers the water wheel at **Bickleigh Mill** to drive the internal milling machinery; the mill has been developed as a popular craft centre where craftsmen and women can be seen in action, working at pottery, spinning, leatherwork, jewellery and corn-dolly making. The adjacent 19th-century farm, stocked with rare and traditional breeds, uses its splendid shire horses and oxen for power. Hand-milking of cows and goats can be seen daily. Within the farm a museum depicts Devon rural life at the turn of the century.

Across the river from the village, **Bickleigh Castle**, so called, was a moated and fortified manor house; the gatehouse and small thatched chapel, said to be the oldest complete building in Devon, date from the Norman period and they survived the destruction that followed the Civil War. The Carew family acquired Bickleigh in the early 16th century, establishing an interesting link with Henry VIII's famous flagship, the Mary Rose; it was Admiral Sir George Carew who commanded the ship on her fateful voyage into the Solent, and who drowned with his men when the ship capsized and sank. Visitors today are invited to experience 900 years of history from the earliest features of the buildings through to the largest collection of Second World War original spy and escape gadgets.

Tracing the valley of the River Exe the A396 continues to **Tiverton**.

Tiverton was referred to in King Alfred's will as 'Twyfyrde', 'double ford'; its strategic site was reached by fords over the Rivers Exe and Loman, which join just below the town. It was probably founded as a Saxon settlement in the 7th century; and grew under the protection of the castle built by Richard de Redvers in the early years of the 12th century.

The Earls of Devon occupied Tiverton Castle until the 16th century; by then the woollen industry was well established and particularly the manufacture of kersey, coarse ribbed cloth woven from long wool. One wool merchant, Peter Blundell, founded Blundell's School in 1599; the Old School, built in 1604, still stands near the Loman Bridge at the south-east end of town. R D Blackmore was educated here, and used the triangular lawn as the setting for a fight between John Ridd and Robin Snell in *Lorna Doone*.

Another benefactor, John Greenway, began life as a poor weaver here; he made his fortune and enhanced the Parish Church with the Greenway Chapel, off the entrance porch; the vaulted ceiling is richly embossed with carved stone finials; prayers for his soul are cut in the walls and he is portrayed over a doorway together with his wife. In the town, his alms-houses, though rebuilt, still shelter the elderly.

Bickleigh Castle

*Have grace, ye men, and ever pray
For the soul of John and Joan Greenway.*

Also in the church, notice the painted plaster Lion and Unicorn, thought to date from c1615, marking the Mayor's seat, at the head of the civic pews.

In the 19th century Tiverton survived the demise of the woollen industry through the introduction of lace-making by John Heathcoat; as the inventor of the bobbinette lace machine, he was forced to leave his factory in Leicester after the Luddite riots. He and a handful of key workers settled in the town and opened a new factory in a disused woollen mill on the banks of the Exe.

Today Tiverton is a busy shopping centre and market town; in the centre of the commercial area, between St Peter Street and Bampton Street, the covered market specialises in the products from the region, with individual stalls of butter and cream, fresh fruit, vegetables, poultry and eggs; it is a lively and colourful scene.

Tiverton Museum, in St Andrew Street, is one of the most comprehensive local museums in the county; its collections and displays range from the 'Tivvy Bumper', a steam loco that ran the Exe valley line until its closure, to local wildlife; the museum is open throughout the year and is run by volunteers.

Since 1971, another local preservation society has been working on the restoration of the **Grand Western Canal**; the Burlescombe to Tiverton branch opened in 1814, followed, 24 years later, by a narrower extension to Taunton; the target, of connecting the Bristol Channel with the south coast at Topsham, was never achieved. From the terminus at Tiverton Basin, on Canal Hill, a horse-drawn passenger service operates once again, following a glorious route through unspoilt countryside. A couple of miles north of Tiverton **Knightshayes**

Tiverton Castle

Court is the property of the National Trust; the garden is one of the most beautiful in Devon, fine specimen trees, formal terraces with amusing topiary, woodland garden with rare shrubs and plants all providing a lovely setting for the fine Victorian mansion designed by William Burges. The azaleas and rhododendrons are especially fine.

Back towards Tiverton take the A373 eastbound; cross the M5 and follow the signs to **Uffculme**. A large village on the River Culm, which was an important centre for the wool trade, exporting serges to Holland, Uffculme's surviving woollen mill at Coldharbour to the west of the village closed down in 1981 but was then converted into a Working Wool Museum. Visitors can watch the full range of woollen and worsted manufacture – the great heaving and clanking looms chattering away in demonstration production. The wool and cloth made up on the machines can be bought in lengths and in garments. Other attractions include a weaver's cottage, dye and carpenters' workshop, the water-wheel and steam engine and a picnic area beside the mill leat.

The mill was built as a grist mill in 1753 after a great flood which destroyed the previous building; in 1797 it was purchased by Thomas Fox, a Quaker woollen manufacturer from nearby Wellington (Somerset), who needed water power for the expansion of his business. He added the imposing red brick and stone factory which has been used for the manufacture of serge, flannel and worsted yarn by Fox Brothers for nearly two centuries.

The parish church, St Mary's, is mainly 15th century, but the tower and spire were rebuilt in the 19th century. The church is noted for having the longest rood-screen in Devon; it is also one of the earliest, c1400. Take the B3391 to Willand and follow signs to **Cullompton**, 2½ miles south. The main road between Exeter and Taunton used to drive its way through

Tiverton Castle
Dominating the River Exe, the castle dates from 1106, and its dull exterior belies much of interest within. The circular Norman south-east tower has survived – originally there were four – and it houses an extensive clock collection. There is a medieval gatehouse, with 5ft thick walls, and a ruined 13th-century chapel; the castle boasts one of the finest collections of Civil War armour in the country. Originally moated on three sides, with the Exe on the fourth, it extended well into the surrounding town; part of the road opposite the main gate is known as 'The Works', indicating the 'outworks' of the castle. In place of the moat between the castle and the church there is now an avenue of fine chestnuts. A key Royalist stronghold during the Civil War, it fell in 1645 to the Roundheads, whose General, Sir Thomas Fairfax, destroyed the main fortifications to the west, thus ending its military importance.

The Devil's Footprints
February 1853 was cold and snow lay on the ground along the Exe estuary; on the night of the 8th someone, or something, left a trail of footprints that covered over 100 miles. From Teignmouth to Exmouth, through villages, across fields, over walls and on the roofs of houses, into locked enclosures the footprints wandered with no apparent purpose or logic.

They were described as hooflike, even cloven-hoofed, and were of a two-legged beast, with a stride of about 16 inches. The following day the men of the area searched for the beast with shotguns and cudgels, and the news spread as far as London where *The Times* and the *Illustrated London News* printed articles which began a long correspondence trying to explain the strange occurrence. Many creatures were suggested; badgers, bustards, rats and cats, and even kangaroos, but no definitive answer was forthcoming, and so the trail was christened 'The Devil's Footprints'.

Cullompton High Street, but now the M5 carries all but local traffic. It is a bright little market town consisting of one main street, variously Fore Street, High Street and Upper High Street, with narrow 'courts' and lanes running off.

Cullompton was one of the great woollen manufacturing towns of Devon; Daniel Defoe listed Cullompton with Tiverton and Bampton 'and all the north east part of the county which . . . is . . . fully employed, the people made rich, and the poor that are properly so called, well subsisted, and employed by it [woollen manufacturing].' Such prosperity is conspicuous in the magnificent parish church, St Andrew's, tucked away in a 'close', off the main street.

There was a collegiate church on this site before the Norman Conquest, but the present building dates from c1430; the west tower, 100ft tall, in red sandstone with white Beer stone pinnacles and carvings is the town's landmark. Inside, the wagon roof is richly gilded and decorated against a faded blue background; there is a Jacobean gallery in oak, one of the longest in Devon, and a brightly painted rood screen. The south aisle was added in the 1520s by John Lane, a clothier, to rival a similar aisle built by his friend John Greenway at St Peter's, Tiverton; the roof is superbly fan-vaulted, and there are carvings of sheep shears, a teasel holder, and John Lane's merchant's mark. A rare survival, displayed in the aisle, is the 'Golgotha' or 'Calvary', which originally stood on the rood-loft: a great tree-trunk rudely carved with skulls, bones and foliage. The Charities list, by the west door, includes 'Weaver Wood's gift . . . to poor men and women' and Melhuish's gift of the rents from a tenement to be distributed 'in shirts to poor men'. In Fore Street, the Manor House Hotel is Elizabethan, with an elaborate 'shell' arch over the door, and next door The

Walronds is an unusual town house, two wings on either side of a cobbled courtyard. The town suffered disastrous fires, notably the Great Fire of 1839, so the majority of other buildings are Victorian – there are some interesting buildings in red brick, like the Pound Square Chapel, with moulded details.

In the 'courts', cottage and craft industries have sprung up like ninepins – pine-stripping, furniture restoration, engineering workshops and a host of new ventures; on the east side the passageways lead on past vegetable plots to the river. The Showman pub, on Station Road, was formerly the Station Inn; its name was changed in 1971 to mark the use of the adjoining site by members of the Showman's Guild – there is a fascinating working model of a Showman's Steam Engine in the lounge.

South of Cullompton and towards Exeter, on minor roads and tucked away quietly in the heart of the countryside, the villages of **Bradninch** and **Silverton** are particularly attractive. Silverton's medieval church tower dominates the network of village streets; there are some fine Georgian houses and earlier cottages. One of the Leach family, potters descended from Bernard Leach, works in the village.

Torquay

Population: 57,491

Early Closing: Wed

Cashpoints: *Barclays* 39 Fleet St; *Lloyds* 45 Union St, 260/262 Union St, 1 Vaughan Parade; *Midland* 4 Strand; *NatWest* 15 Strand

Tourist Information: Vaughan Parade

Attractions: Babbacombe Model Village, Bygones Museum, Kents Cavern, Torquay Museum, Torre Abbey*

Arts: Babbacombe Theatre, Princess Theatre

Leisure: English Riviera Centre, Torquay Swimming Pool

Cinemas: Odeon

By Road: London 194 miles (A380, M5, M4), Plymouth 35 miles (A379, A385, A38)

By Rail: 2hrs 50mins from London (on a branch of the London, Paddington to Penzance line). Direct services to Exeter and Paignton. Connections to Plymouth via Newton Abbot.

2 Torbay and the South Hams

The most popular image of Devon as a holiday destination is epitomised in the promotion of Torbay as the English Riviera: posters create an image of a sub-tropical, palm-waving paradise with perpetually blue skies and apparently warm seas. Without doubt it is this area of Devon, from the Exe estuary southwards to Dartmouth and Kingsbridge, and including the Mecca of Torbay, that attracts the majority of the summer visitors.

The coastline here faces east, so is sheltered from the prevailing winds, and around many of the most favoured spots encircling hills provide additional protection, creating cosy microclimates. Torquay took off in the 18th century as a good place to stay, helpfully promoted by the impossibility of travelling on the continent during the Napoleonic Wars. As tastes have changed and facilities improved, other resorts have developed to attract tourists.

Outside the resorts much of the coastline has, thankfully, remained untamed and unmarred thanks to the protection of the National Trust and the South Devon Heritage Coast Service; Berry Head and Sharkham Point, west of Brixham, and Start Point and Prawle Point at the southern end of Start Bay, offer wild wind-swept walking and magnificent sea views.

The sheltered and wooded estuary of the Dart, dotted with small craft and bordered by picturesque villages remains unspoilt, as does the Kingsbridge estuary; and venture inland to discover the rich rolling countryside of the South Hams, 'the frutefullest part of all Devonshire'. Between Totnes and Kingsbridge the dense network of lanes is cut deep between thick ancient hedges; a well wooded landscape of ruddy red soil, cob cottages and farmhouses, scones and crusty Devonshire cream. This is cider country, and in September the branches of trees in the orchards bend to the ground under the weight of the crop. Red Devon cattle, almost matching the fiery earth, are giving way to the ubiquitous Friesian herds.

Of the towns, Newton Abbot, Totnes and Kingsbridge are important market centres, each at the head of an estuary and commanding a broad hinterland of agricultural production.

TORQUAY

Torquay claims to be the sophisticated playground of the English Riviera, comparable with Monte Carlo or Cannes. Amongst its attractions it boasts an extensive leisure and conference complex called the English Riviera Centre; certainly its palm trees are real enough and the night life as exciting and varied as anywhere. An historical travel writer said of Torquay: 'It is not England, but a bit of sunny Italy taken bodily from its rugged coast and placed here amid the green lanes and the pleasant pastoral lands of beautiful Devon.'

The terraces and villas of the town follow the contours of the hills that ring the harbour, bobbing with pleasure boats; it is sheltered on all sides except due south and that faces the pleasant sweep of Torbay, with Paignton and Brixham on the adjacent shores. Its balmy climate has attracted summer sun-seekers and winter patients since the early 19th century, but before that there was little here besides a sprinkling of fishermen's cottages around the quay.

A short tour of the town on foot can begin at the Pavilion, beside the harbour; the Pavilion, recently refurbished to house shops and a restaurant, was originally opened in 1912 as a ballroom and assembly hall. It was nicknamed 'the White Palace'; the design has an eastern flavour with green copper domes and a tiled exterior surface. The municipal orchestra performed here for 25 years under

Kents Cavern
A mysterious world of underground caves and galleries, Kents Cavern has provided archaeologists with some of the earliest evidence of man's presence in England. The site is on the east side of the Hope's Nose headland in Torquay and can be reached either by the Babbacombe Road or Meadfoot Road.

Since the 16th century, visitors have been attracted to the caves to marvel at the stalactites and stalagmites; it was not until 1824 that some fossil bones and flint implements were found by a priest, but the implication that man might pre-date the creation story was too revolutionary a thought for that time and he never publicised his finds.

Later in the 19th century, William Pengelly, the founder of the Torquay Natural History Society, began to explore the caves in detail and unearthed layer upon layer of evidence of human and animal habitation covering nearly half a million years. Excavations beneath the stalagmites revealed a world of cave-dwellers, in an untamed landscape populated by sabre-toothed tigers, mammoths and bears, and a whole bear skeleton has been found. Today Kents Cavern is a popular visitor attraction and the Torquay Museum has a permanent exhibition illustrating the various layers and what they reveal about life in the prehistoric past.

John 'Babbacombe' Lee
John Lee was accused of murder on 14 November 1884, when Miss Emma Keyse of The Glen, Babbacombe, on the north-east edge of Torquay, was hit over the head with a hatchet and her throat cut. Lee worked as a servant in her house and was the only man present when the body was found. Although the evidence was purely circumstantial, he was sentenced to death. He was twenty years of age.

On 23rd February 1885, Lee was sent to the gallows at Exeter gaol; the hangman released the trapdoor, but it stuck fast after moving just a few inches. The warders stamped on it but it would not move, and Lee was taken away while the mechanism was tested. It was found to be working, and they tried again. For the second time the trapdoor stuck, the warders stamped to no avail, and Lee was removed. They tried for a third time but the same thing happened. The prison chaplain then intervened and said that the law stated that they could only try three times, and although this was not true, the outcry led to Lee's sentence being commuted to life imprisonment. He served 22 years and then returned to his home in Abbotskerswell. He later became a publican in London.

conductors as famous as Sir Henry Wood, Sir Edward Elgar and Sir Landon Ronald. Behind the Pavilion the great limestone cliff and gardens are floodlit at night.

Follow the seafront walk westwards to Abbey Sands; the great green sward behind leads to Torre Abbey, founded in 1196; considerable remains are preserved within the brightly blooming municiple gardens, including the 12th-century entrance to the chapter house, the 19th-century gatehouse, the guest hall, and most impressive of all, the Great Barn – locally it is known as the Spanish barn, because about 400 prisoners from the Armada were brought here from a captured Spanish ship. The present house at Torre Abbey is 17th- and 18th-century in date and was the home of the Cary family; it now serves as the town's art gallery.

The Carys and their local rivals, the Palks, determined much of the careful planning of the town's development in the 19th century: Sir Lawrence Palk in particular set out to attract an upper-class clientele, and built appropriately elegant and spacious villas to accommodate them; Croft Road and Warren Road circling the hill overlooking the harbour contain some fine examples of luxurious villas. Abbey Road leads into Fleet Street, the principal shopping thoroughfare, to the Strand. It was Sir Lawrence Palk who began the construction of the inner harbour and the terraces of lodging houses, on the north and east sides, for genteel families. Above the modern and often garish shopfronts of Victoria Parade are some elaborate and well-preserved 19th-century façades. On summer evenings the shops here stay open late into the night, giving the place that continental feel with strolling holiday-makers mingling with the locals, and coloured lights fringing the bay.

East of the harbour the cliffs rise up to Daddy Hole Plain: the great chasm in the cliff where the Plain meets the sea was attributed to

'Daddy' – the Devil. The views over the bay are superb, and further east through Lincombe Gardens, at Meadfoot, the way continues past Thatcher Stone, an isolated craggy rock ¼ mile off shore, to the point at Hope's Nose. The A379 follows the coast south from Torquay, past hotels and guest houses, to Paignton; go north for Babbacombe's beaches and model village.

Paignton lies at the centre of Torbay, facing east, straight out to sea. It is sheltered on the landward side by the rich rolling country-side of south-east Devon, with its fiery red soil. Saxon colonists founded a village here and by the Norman conquest it was in the possession of the Bishop of Exeter, who had a palace near the church. Surviving remnants of the medieval village can still be seen in Church Street and Kirkham Street. Kirkham House, open to the public, was the 15th-century home of a prosperous merchant or perhaps an official from the Bishop's palace; it houses an exhibition by artists and craftsmen including modern furniture, tapestries and pottery.

A hundred years ago Paignton was described as 'a neat and improving village and bathing place' which had 'risen into notice as a place of resort for invalids during the last 15 years, and is still capable of being made a first-rate watering place . . .' But it was still a farming parish, noted for its cider and its very large and sweet flatpole cabbages, called 'Paignton cabbages'.

The railway reached the village in 1859, and from then on its success as a seaside resort was assured: new roads and new villas were built, not only for summer visitors, but also for an increasing number of permanent residents who chose to take advantage of the area's sheltered aspect and mild climate.

Paignton has one great asset over its popular and fashionable neighbour, Torquay: its beach; in fact there are two beaches, separated by the appropriately named Redcliffe

Torquay Museum
'Eighteen gentlemen' founded the Torquay Natural History Society in 1844 and from that initiative a museum gradually developed. The present purpose-built building was erected in 1875. From the Clock Tower on the Strand by the inner harbour, the museum is five minutes walk up Torwood Street.

The exhibition of local and regional geology illustrates the development of the landscape and life around Torbay over the past 400 million years; it includes sections on the formation of Dartmoor's famous tors, the China Clay industry, fossils and corals. The archaeological displays are rich, too, as many of the earliest and best finds from Kents Cavern are shown here: cases show the surviving evidence for hyena, lions, bears, sabre-toothed tigers and woolly rhinos that once roamed the area, as well as the primitive tools and weapons chiselled out of rock by man. The Laycock Gallery on the top floor contains an unexpectedly excellent display of rural life: agricultural tools and farmhouse furniture and ornaments, cooking and kitchen devices, even a distinctively shaped Dartmoor kettle.

Paignton

Population: 40,820

Cashpoints: *Barclays* 6/8
Palace Ave; *Lloyds* 2 Palace
Ave; *Midland* 7 Palace Ave;
NatWest 15 Victoria St

Tourist Information: The
Esplanade

Attractions: Kirkham
House, Oldway, Paignton
and Dartmouth Railway*,
Quaywest beach resort,
Zoological and Botanical
Gardens

Arts: Festival Theatre,
Palace Avenue Theatre

Leisure: Torbay Leisure
Centre

Cinema: Torbay Cinema

By Road: London 198 miles
(A380, M5, M4), Plymouth
34 miles (A385, A38)

By Rail: 3hrs from London
(on a branch of the main
London, Paddington to
Penzance line). Direct
services to Torquay and
Exeter. Connections to
Plymouth via Newton
Abbot

Mending nets

headland. They provide safe sandy bathing,
ideal for families with young children; under
the cliffs the sands are ruddy red, blending to
gold in the flatter open stretches. There is a
family beach resort, Quaywest, and Paignton
also has a zoo with botanical gardens. A
promenade, backed by lawns and gardens,
borders the beaches, with the pier midway
between Redcliffe and the harbour. The little
harbour at the southern end of the town,
tucked under Roundham Head, was built in
1838; although frequently packed with pleasure
craft in the summer it remains a practical
fishing harbour, rich in local colour and the
tangy smells of fresh tar, fishing tackle and
lobster pots.

At the top of Torbay Road, immediately
opposite the Festival Theatre, a pair of old
GWR iron gates marks the entrance to the
Torbay and Dartmouth Steam Railway; from
here the *Torbay Express* or *Lydham Manor* locos
maintain a regular timetable of excursions to
Goodrington Sands, Churston and Kingswear,
linking with the ferry to Dartmouth.

South of Paignton, **Goodrington Sands** and
Broadsands are well-frequented beaches,
Elberry Cove and **Fishcombe Beach** less so.

The town and harbour of **Brixham**, on the
southern horn of the crescent that forms
Torbay, are protected by the promontory of
Berry Head, and by the great arm of the
breakwater that extends nearly ½ mile out to
shelter the port from north and north-easterly
gales.

The old harbour used to extend
considerably further inland, making a natural
anchorage protected on all sides; but it was
infilled and the central part of lower Brixham is
now built over it. The original Saxon
settlement was up by the church in Higher
Brixham.

Today, cottages and small town houses pack
the valley sides of the harbour; by the quayside

pubs, steep steps and narrow alleys thread their way up the hillsides between tiers of terraces.

Life and work have for centuries revolved around the sea; it was always a precarious and dangerous existence, as recalled by a monument in the churchyard to 100 sailors who perished in a storm in 1866, when 40 ships were driven on to the rocks.

By the middle of the 18th century Brixham was sending fish to London, Bath and Exeter; and by the early 19th century it was the most noted wholesale fish market in the west of England. Fish was carried up to 50 miles inland on pack-horses, but the London-bound fish was sent by sea to Portsmouth and thence overland. In 1900 there were more than 300 fishing boats at the port. The arrival of steam trawlers and the radical changes in fishing technique have left a permanent scar on the long tradition of fishing from Brixham; by the end of the Second World War the fishing fleet was practically extinct. On the quay-side in the restored Market House, the British Fisheries Museum, a branch of the National Maritime Museum, illustrates this story with models and diagrams and exhibits. There is also a local museum.

Permanently moored in the harbour is a full-sized replica of the *Golden Hind*, the ship that took Francis Drake around the world between 1577 and 1580. At the southern end of the inner harbour stands the statue of Prince William of Orange, who landed at Brixham in 1688 to claim the English throne from James II; his ship grounded on the harbour mud and a local fisherman named Varwell is said to have leapt into the water and carried the Prince ashore on his shoulders.

East of the town centre, paths lead to **Berry Head**, now a nature reserve where colonies of seabirds nest in the spectacular limestone cliffs. Among the species to be seen are the fulmar,

Compton Castle
Dating mainly from the 14th to the 16th centuries, Compton is one of the few fortified houses to have survived without the alterations and additions which usually modify a building of this age. Situated just outside Torquay in the village of Compton, the exterior appears sturdily defensive, with a portcullis entrance, battlements and machicolations. The house has remained, with only one break, for 600 years in the Gilbert family; it is now owned by the National Trust.

The great hall, complete with screens passage and minstrels' gallery, was rebuilt in the 1950s, faithfully following the medieval plan and using matching materials wherever possible. At the east end are the buttery, pantry and kitchen, and the solar, cellar and chapel are at the west end.

Sir Humphrey Gilbert encouraged Queen Elizabeth I to expand her territory overseas; he rose to fame as the founder of the colony of Newfoundland in 1583. The following year his half-brother, Sir Walter Raleigh, sent off another party to North America; that and subsequent voyages led to the colonisation of Virginia. John Gilbert, Sir Humphrey's eldest son, accompanied Raleigh to Guiana; he was knighted by the Earl of Essex for his bravery during the attack on Cadiz.

Dartmouth

Population: 5,581

Market Days: Tue, Fri

Cashpoints: *Lloyds* 2 Spithead; *NatWest* 2 Duke St

Tourist Information: 11 Duke Street

Attractions: Bayard's Cove Fort, Butterwalk Museum*, Dartmouth Castle, Newcomen Memorial Engine*

By Road: London 215 miles (A379, A3022, A380, M5, M4), Plymouth 30 miles (A379, A3022, A385, A38)

By Rail: The nearest British Rail station is at Paignton (3hrs from London). There are seasonal private steam-hauled services (Torbay and Dartmouth Railway) from Kingswear to Paignton

Dartmouth steam railway

kittiwake, guillemot and shag. Unusual and beautiful wild flowers hug the crevices – white rock rose, navelwort, and pelitory of the wall. Berry Head has been fortified since the Iron Age; the construction of the existing Napoleonic fortifications destroyed traces of a Roman camp. The Guard House inside the fort offers teas and light refreshments. Footpaths continue to St Mary's Bay and Sharkham Point.

DARTMOUTH AND KINGSWEAR

On either side of the estuary, about a mile from the mouth of the River Dart, both towns are dramatically sited on the steep hillsides rising from the water's edge; the houses cling to the slopes, tier above tier, a wonderful backdrop to the boating activity off shore. **Kingswear**, on the west bank, is the railway terminus and embarkation point for the ferry which has plied to and fro from time immemorial. There is scarcely space for the railway station, jammed against the hillside with the road twisting sharply to climb the dizzy incline.

On the opposite bank, **Dartmouth** has successfully expanded onto flat reclaimed land along the valley side and over the Mill Pool which once split the town in two, between the market and the bandstand; but behind the church in the old part of town the cottages remain, perched one above the other, and linked by almost vertical cobbled steps. The New Quay was constructed in the 16th century and the New Ground, north of the little enclosed harbour, in the 17th century. The town was well established as a port by the 12th century when both the Second and Third Crusades assembled and departed from here, and there was considerable trade with Bordeaux and Spain, wine being the chief import. Two houses incredibly, survive from the 14th century – Agincourt House at Lower Ferry and The Cherub in Higher Street.

Agincourt House was a wealthy merchant's residence, close to the quay; it is timber-framed and jettied on two storeys.

Bayards Cove gives the best impression of the old river frontage; the cobbled quay was used as the film-set for *The Onedin Line*. The Pilgrim Fathers put in to this quay (a plaque marks the spot) *en route* from Southampton to the New World in the *Mayflower* and *Speedwell*. The main shopping street, Duke Street, leads into Victoria Street, both on the flat reclaimed land of the Mill Pool; the Butterwalk, shaded under a timber-framed arcade, was built in 1635–40. It was badly damaged by bombs in 1943, but has been beautifully reinstated; it is encrusted with wood carvings and jettied, four storeys high. The 'Old Market', in Victoria Street, throbs into life on Tuesdays and Fridays.

There are impressive castles on both sides of the estuary, towards the mouth and protecting the deep water anchorage; a chain could be drawn between them in times of war. Dartmouth Castle was begun in 1481, and was the most advanced piece of fortification in England, being one of the first castles to be designed specifically for artillery.

The harbour remains very much alive with a busy fishing fleet, the ferries, numerous pleasure boats, cruises, and particularly as the on-the-spot training ground for the Royal Naval College which overlooks the town. Cruisers carry passengers to and from Totnes throughout the season, a beautiful trip through some of the finest river scenery.

From Dartmouth a minor road leads south to the coast at **Start Bay**, a magnificent sweep of sands, shingle and cliffs more than 5 miles long between Combe Point, by the Dart estuary in the north, and Start Point, to the south. The little stone-built village of **Slapton** is about half a mile inland from Slapton Sands – so called, although they are in fact a shingle

Thomas Newcomen
Proclaimed as the man who saved the mines of Devon, Newcomen, together with Thomas Savery, invented and patented the first atmospheric steam engine. Steam was injected into a cylinder that raised a piston which descended under gravity for its power stroke.

By the end of the 17th century many of the mines in Devon and Cornwall had been driven so deep that it became impossible to prevent them from flooding; Newcomen's engine could pump them clear of water, prolonging the lives of each mine until the mineral seams were worked out.

Born in Dartmouth in 1663, Newcomen was an ironmonger. He developed his trade and skill to produce pumping engines that revolutionised the mining technology of his day; a tribute to his skill is the fact that some of his engines were still working 200 years after they were built.

James Watt, when repairing one of Newcomen's engines, realised that if the cylinder was sealed from the air, and the steam was used to create the power, then the pressure was even greater, and this led to the invention of the steam engine as we know it. A working example of one of Newcomen's engines can be seen at Dartmouth, in the Engine House by Mayor's Avenue Car Park.

Hallsands

Protected from the sea by a shingle foreshore, the small village of Hallsands nestled under towering red cliffs. Early this century, a small thriving community of fishermen lived in twenty-nine houses that constituted the village.

In 1897 permission was given to a contractor to dredge the shingle bank, and 650,000 tons of gravel were removed. The resulting gradual drop in the level of the beach left the houses unnaturally exposed. As a direct result, in 1903 part of the road collapsed, and several houses were undermined. Petitions from the locals prompted denial of responsibility from the contractor concerned. An attempt at reparation was made by the building of a retaining sea wall, totally inadequate against the ferocious south-westerly gales that battered the little houses. A severe storm in the winter of 1917, raging for four days and nights, rendered all but one uninhabitable.

Standing securely on the high cliff-top above, Trouts Hotel, now flats, is a symbol of the stoicism and hard work of two sisters, Ella and Patience Trout, who lost their home in the storm. In the same year they rescued an American seaman from a sinking ship. Ella was awarded the OBE, and the sailor's parents were so grateful that they sent money which the sisters used to start work on the hotel, which they built themselves.

ridge more or less in the middle of the bay; the ridge encloses a remarkable freshwater lake, Slapton Ley.

It is an attractive village, sheltered in a hollow of the South Hams hills, and renowned for the early production of garden crops; farming and horticulture are the main activities of the area. The narrow and twisting village street almost circles the church; from the triangle of pretty cottages to the south a cobbled path leads up to the lych gate. Inside the main (north) porch the Sanctuary Ring allowed a criminal to elude justice by claiming sanctuary under the canon law; he had to make his confession and then leave the kingdom by the shortest route to the coast. The church spire is medieval, dating from the 14th century.

Slapton Ley has been designated a Site of Special Scientific Interest; the reed beds are a rare habitat in the south west and attract visiting wild fowl to roost in the winter. Mallard breed on the Ley, red-faced coot are regularly seen, and the great crested grebe, once almost wiped out by the Victorian fashion trade, is back. The woodlands fringing the Ley are semi-natural, in spring speckled with buds and the spikes of yellow iris.

At the centre of the shingle ridge a granite obelisk commemorates the evacuation of Slapton village and much of the surrounding area in 1943 to provide a live-ammunition battle-practice area for the assault on Normandy in June 1944; the Sherman tank in the car-park at **Torcross** is a similar memorial, but this to those United States troops whose lives were lost in the practice.

At Torcross the road veers inland, so to complete the arc of the bay one must continue on foot; the coastal footpath follows the shore to Start Point. It is a magnificent walk with the steep cliffs of the Point jutting out precipitously into the sea. Past Beesands and Tinseys Head the beach peters out and is replaced, at a slightly higher level, by a rock ledge; a handful of dejected ruins sit on the ledge – the remains of the once thriving village of **Hallsands**.

The cliffs at the Point are over 100ft high, on the south side almost sheer and streaked by quartz veins running through the dark rock. The path follows the northern and more sheltered side of the ridge to the lighthouse at the very tip.

KINGSBRIDGE

Kingsbridge is known as the capital of the South Hams, a rich agricultural region at the head of a five-mile navigable inlet of the sea, Kingsbridge estuary.

St Edmund's Church, towards the top of Fore Street, behind the Shambles, is largely 13th century; one of the most interesting monuments is an exquisite marble relief, by John Flaxman, commemorating Frances Schutz Drury, who died in 1817 on her way home from Bombay. Notice the inscription outside the priest's door.

Fore Street runs from the quayside up the hill, neatly bisecting the ridge, and flanked on either side by houses.

The granite piers of the Shambles were originally erected in 1586 to make a single-storey corn market arcade; this was replaced in the 18th century by the butchers' shambles which still stands, though now converted to a coffee shop. Farther up the street on the left is the Cookworthy Museum.

At **Woodleigh**, just off the B3196, the Woodland Trust manages a light-dappled stretch of woods on the banks of the River Avon; it includes Woodleigh, Titcombe and part of Bedlime Woods, with the disused railway line from South Brent to Kingsbridge running alongside.

River Maid Launches link Kingsbridge with **Salcombe**, nearer the mouth of the estuary, or

Cookworthy Museum, Kingsbridge

Just above the junction with Duncombe Street, the Cookworthy Museum is housed in Kingsbridge's old Grammar School, endowed by Thomas Crispin; the school was opened in 1670 and admitted 12 boys 'in suits of grey frieze cloth'.

The museum illustrates life in South Devon with artefacts, costumes, local photographs, toys and dolls which are displayed in the schoolroom, its original panelling inscribed with schoolboy graffiti. A Victorian pharmacy occupies the Duncombe Room, and the school kitchen has been remodelled to represent that of a Victorian farmhouse kitchen, with all manner of culinary devices. Larger agricultural equipment, vehicles and barn machinery feature in the Farm Gallery.

The museum is named after William Cookworthy (1705–1780) who was born in Kingsbridge; a Quaker, he worked as an apothecary in Plymouth where he met traders from the Far East who brought back porcelain from China. He identified the china clays of Cornwall as 'kaolin', the basic ingredient of porcelain, and succeeded in making the first true English hard-paste porcelain at a factory in Plymouth. The production of china never developed in Devon because of the lack of coal: it was easier to transport the clay to the coal than vice versa. But China clay is still quarried and exported from Plymouth.

Newton Abbot

Population: 20,744

Early Closing: Thu

Market Day: Sat

Cashpoints: *Barclays* 40
Courtenay St; *Lloyds* 41
Courtenay St; *Midland* 42
Courtenay St; *NatWest* 48
Courtenay St

Tourist Information: 8
Sherborne Rd

Attractions: Bradley
Manor*

Leisure: Dyron's Sports
Centre, Kingsteignton
Swimming Pool

By Road: London 188 miles
(A380, A38, M5, M4),
Exeter 16 miles (A380)

By Rail: 2hrs 30mins from
London (London,
Paddington to Penzance
line). Direct services to
Paignton, Plymouth,
Teignmouth and Torquay.
Connections to Exmouth
via Exeter.

*St Leonard's Tower,
Newton Abbot*

follow the A381; the hairpin bends down into
the town rival those of an alpine track.
Salcombe is Devon's southernmost resort,
boasting a superbly mild climate; the port
shelters on the steep west bank of the
Kingsbridge estuary scarcely a mile from the
open sea.

For centuries Salcombe was a fishing town
with a handful of shipwright's yards and a
scatter of cottages clinging to the valley slopes;
the event of the year was the Whitsun fair.
Towards the end of the 18th century visitors
and those seeking quiet retirement sought out
Salcombe, a development spurred on by the
arrival of the railway at Kingsbridge in 1893.
Cottages, villas and hotels were spawned on
the hillside, linked by zig-zag bends to
negotiate the difficult contours; it is a
wonderfully picturesque setting, and despite
the modern building remains full of maritime
flavour.

On the opposite shore, at **East Portlemouth**,
landlubbers can enjoy the sandy bays – Smalls
Cove, Sunny Cove and Mill Bay, using the
passenger ferry to cross the narrow stretch of
sparkling water from the steps near the Ferry
Inn. Salcombe's museum of maritime and local
history at Custom House Quay illustrates local
trades and industry as well as mementos from
the Second World War battle-training ground
at Slapton. The South Devon Coastal footpath
continues from Salcombe to Bolt Head, Bolt
Tail and Bigbury Bay; sheer cliffs tumbling to
the wave-battered shore for the first stretch,
followed by sand dunes and rippled flats at
low tide at Thurlestone and Bantham.

On the east side of the estuary, through
East Portlemouth to the little village of East
Prawle; from here a single track lane twists and
turns through high-hedged fields to a
convenient car park about half a mile from
Prawle Point. This is the southernmost
extremity of Devon, flanked by some of the

finest stretches of coastal scenery. The South-west Coastal Footpath heads east to Lannacombe and Start Point and west to Gara Rock and East Portlemouth, almost entirely under the auspices of the National Trust.

NEWTON ABBOT

At the head of the Teign estuary, **Newton Abbot** straddles the River Lemon which enters the Teign just below the town. Fishing locally has been both a popular pastime and commercial activity:

The Teign for Salmon, the Dart for Peel,
Fort Leat for Trout and the Lemon for Eel.

In the 13th century the abbot of Torre Abbey founded a 'new town' on the south bank of the river, while Sir Theobald de Englishville, lord of the manor on the north side, established a borough known as Newton Bushel, with a market and fair. Both prospered and eventually grew together to become known as Newton Abbot.

The symbol and centre of the town, the ancient tower of St Leonard, is at the crossroads of Courtenay Street, East Street, Bank Street and Wolborough Street; the chapel that once adjoined it was demolished in 1836. Beside the tower, the first declaration of William III, Prince of Orange, 'the glorious defender of the Protestant religion and the liberties of England', was read in November 1688, as he made his way from Brixham to London. Prince William stayed at Forde House and his army, of 30,000 men, camped on Milber Down.

Newton Abbot has long been a route centre – first on the main road between Exeter and Dartmouth; later the Stover Canal brought granite from Haytor and ball clay from the Bovey Basin through the town; and in 1846, the railway arrived. Newton's position, at the head of the estuary and at the meeting place of

Prawle Point and Start Point
Prawle Point, four miles south-east of Salcombe, forms the southernmost tip of Devon; it is lashed by the full fury of the waves in stormy weather and has been chiselled and chipped into an almost vertical drop beneath the Coastguard look-out station. The craggy cliffs are decorated with sea pinks, and gulls nest in the crevices. Off-shore the yachts edge their way carefully out beyond the protection of the headland or seek shelter on the east-facing lee coast of Start Bay.

From East Prawle a high-banked twisting lane leads to a car park conveniently close to the cliff; the walks and sea views are magnificent.

Eastwards, the path follows the raised beach, with rocky coves and coarse shingle beaches below, past Langerstone and Peartree Point to Ravens Cove; and then out to the lighthouse at Start Point with a great vista to the north.

Just off Start Point, the wreck of the *SS Medina*, sunk by a German torpedo in 1917, has attracted fortune seekers; she was carrying a cargo of crates of ancient Indian artefacts, the property of Lord Carmichael, who had been governor of Victoria (Australia), Madras and Bengal, consecutively, and was bringing gifts from Indian Maharajas to the British Crown. In 1987, working at a depth of 200 feet, in black silt-laden water, divers began to recover some of the fabulous treasure.

Bradley Manor, Newton Abbot

Bradley is a National Trust property with 70 acres of woodland and meadow in Bradley Vale at the north-west end of Newton Abbot; the River Lemon flows through the estate, as does the Bradley Leat, an old mill stream. The manor house itself sinks into the surrounding cushion of woodland; the earliest and central portion of the house dates from the 13th century, though generally it is of 15th-century construction.

The hall and screens passage follow the classic medieval pattern; the fireplace is magnificent, hewn from three great slabs of moor stone. In the ante-chapel notice the little opening just inside the door from the porch that is thought to have been for the use of the 15th century cat. The chapel was built in 1427; the carved bosses of the barrel roof bear the arms of local families associated with the house, and one, of a bearded head, is said to represent God. The altar stone, removed and split for use as gate posts at the dissolution, was found and restored to its proper position in 1927.

The old kitchen originally had a cobbled floor; the fireplace survives – the granite surrounds are reckoned to weigh four tons. Upstairs the Fleur-de-Lys room has the feature of stencilled decoration on the walls and a striped painted 'curtain' by the window – all dating from about 1500.

several valleys, made it a natural junction, and branch lines were opened to Torbay (1848) and Moretonhampstead (1866–1959). The town became the centre of the GWR locomotive and carriage repair works, employing more than 600 people. Much of the town was laid out at this time to house the railway workforce in neat terraces; more stylish Italianate villas were planned and built in Courtenay Park and Devon Square by the Courtenays who owned much of the site.

On Wednesdays and Saturdays the market hall behind the Alexandra Cinema is packed with stalls of local produce, bric-à-brac and clothes; the livestock market prospers, although the buying and selling of sheep and pigs now takes place in the shadow of a multi-storey car park.

From Newton Abbot take the B3195 to Kingsteignton, then the A381, along the shore of the estuary, to **Teignmouth**. It is a pleasant seaside town built on the north side of the mouth of the Teign estuary. Originally a sandy wasteland extended from the northern shore leaving only a narrow channel, between the Point and the cliffs of Shaldon on the opposite bank, the Ness. In the 18th and 19th centuries, this rough ground was developed, as the popularity of the resort attracted increasing numbers of visitors. The narrow channel, through which boats gain access to the shelter of the estuary or to dock at the quay-side, is scoured daily by the tide and the river; the currents are fast and strong and the sand bars so treacherous to shipping that all cargo vessels entering or leaving the port are navigated through by Trinity House pilots.

The west side of the bar, facing up the estuary, is full of the character of old Teignmouth; here were the boat-building yards and rope walks. From the quays, international trade continues to flourish under the eye of the customs-house.

A passenger ferry runs between the River Beach, on the west side of the bar, and Shaldon; the ferry's livery, black and white below the gunwales, is believed to date from the 16th century. In the late 18th and early 19th centuries Teignmouth became a fashionable seaside resort; John Keats came here to nurse his dying brother and fell in love with the Devon countryside; he resided in Northumberland Place at the house now known as Keats' House. The town retains a good deal of its late-Georgian and early-Victorian architecture, particularly the elegant terraces and crescents of Powderham Terrace and the Den which was laid out with a carriageway and lawn; the Assembly Rooms, now the cinema, were built in 1826. The Esplanade, along the seafront, extends for nearly 2 miles; at the northern end a path continues beside the railway line. The Pier, built in the 1860s, once marked the segregation point between male and female bathers; from the end of the Pier, steamers carried passengers to Exmouth, Plymouth and Bournemouth; today it houses an amusement arcade and sweet shops. A wooden bridge was built across the Teign estuary in 1826–7; users were charged a toll of 1d. It was rebuilt in 1931 in reinforced concrete and steel, and the collection of tolls ceased in 1948; the bridge and toll house are listed buildings.

With a sprinkling of guest houses and no large hotels, **Shaldon** remains relatively untouched by the annual invasion of summer visitors. Its narrow lanes deter heavy traffic. Within the maze of streets are a wealth of charming Georgian and Victorian houses and cottages; those around the bowling green are particularly attractive, including the London Inn. The beach, being close to the tidal channel, can be dangerous for swimming, so tends to attract sailors rather than swimmers.

North of Teignmouth the A379 coast road

Forde House

Ninety-two rabbits, 69 partridges, 48 lobsters, 37 turkeys, 11 curlews, 21½ dozen larks and 6 oxen, washed down with two hogsheads of beer and 35 quarts of white wine – just part of the fare consumed by Charles I and his retinue at Forde house in 1625. Surely a less indulgent feast was enjoyed by Oliver Cromwell who visited 20 years later on his way to attack Dartmouth.

Forde House, on the south-east edge of Newton Abbot, was built on an E-shaped plan by Sir Richard Reynell in 1610, adjoining an earlier manorial house. Finely carved panelling, oak staircases and doors, and magnificent plaster ceilings are features of the house; but the history of its auspicious guests gives the house its greatest interest.

Another visitor was William of Orange, who found the owner, Sir William Courtenay, 'not at home' presumably so that if William's mission to restore Protestant authority in England failed he would not have to face any retribution. He had left instructions that food and accommodation should be provided, and the room William stayed in, above the porch, has since been known as the 'Orange Room' and has always been decorated in that colour.

Atmospheric Railway Museum

Right on the shoreline at Starcross on the Exe estuary, where the mainline railway still rushes past en route from Exeter to Penzance, an old red stone pumping station, a relic of the great inventor Isambard Kingdom Brunel, has been converted into a unique private museum.

Brunel reckoned that locomotives alone might not be able to haul trains up the steep inclines of the South Devon Railway between Newton Abbot and Exeter. He devised an atmospheric system for the track, consisting of a continuous pipe, laid between the rails, in which ran a piston fitted to the leading vehicle of the train; pumping houses at regular intervals along the line sucked the air out of the pipe, forming a vacuum.

This pumping house is the only one to survive in anything like its original state; it houses an exhibition which includes a working model, using vacuum cleaners to represent the pumping houses, and amazingly a volunteer visitor is propelled up and down the track to demonstrate the effectiveness of the invention.

Unfortunately, in reality, the system was beset with problems, not least that of rats chewing the leather seals on the pipes, and in 1848 it was abandoned with losses in the region of half a million pounds.

leads to **Dawlish**, another pretty seaside resort, once genteel and select enough to have attracted both Jane Austen and Charles Dickens. The first houses were not built on the Strand until 1803, but within a few years the sea front, cliffs and valley sides were transformed by neat rows of sedate villas and boarding houses.

At the centre of the town, the Lawn was left undeveloped as a pleasant open space around a bubbling stream. Now the gardens are planted with rose borders and colourful annuals fill the beds at the roadside to splash the street scene with vivid red, orange and yellow flowers. Ducks and the famous Dawlish Black Swans, from Australia, paddle gracefully up and down the stream and clamber out to waddle about the grassy banks.

The sea is hidden from view by the railway which arrived in 1846; Brunel's line follows the coast, from the Exe estuary right down to Newton Abbot, and here it crosses the sea-front on a granite viaduct, with an arch leading to the beach. The station itself is a fine period-piece, an attraction in its own right.

The beach, over a mile long, is a mixture of sand and red shingle; on either side, craggy red cliffs rise almost vertically from the sea and close down the railway from time to time in winter, as chunks frequently collapse during bad storms. Nevertheless, views of sea and estuary from this stretch of the line are magnificent.

The old village was up by the church, nearly a mile inland, to be safe from raiders; a handful of thatched cottages survive. Elsewhere the gracious villas are white-painted, with stained glass and tiles in the halls and decorative wrought iron balconies. Smaller terraced houses and modern housing estates have infilled old gardens and the steeper slopes – in recent years Dawlish has become a popular place for retirement.

Continuing northwards, a minor road to the right off the A379 is signposted to **Dawlish Warren**; the Warren is a sandy spit that extends over a mile across the mouth of the Exe estuary, almost blocking the river's exit to the sea; an early guide book compared the Warren to a desert, where 'there is not a single oasis' and it remains a wild area today, bleak and windy in winter but a perfect paradise for families on a sultry summer's day. All the commercial amenities are near the railway station: camp sites, caravan parks, ice-cream vendors, pubs and hotels, as well as seaside gift shops bulging with buckets and rubber rings; but even on the busiest days there is plenty of room for everyone and the crowds rapidly thin out towards the northern end of the spit. Part of the area has been designated a nature reserve for the protection of wildlife; bird watchers stalk the reeds for winter migrants and the freshwater ponds are a natural haven for small birds. In early summer the wild orchids carpet the undergrowth.

Two miles north on the A379, at the village of **Starcross**, Brunel's old pumping house has been opened to the public to show his invention of the atmospheric railway.

From Starcross take the B3381 up the steep and darkly wooded slopes of the Haldon Hills; there are pleasant picnic spots and woodland walks with vistas out over the Exe estuary, or eastwards out to sea. Cross the dual carriageways of the A380 to **Chudleigh**. Midway between Exeter and Newton Abbot, Chudleigh was once bisected by the main through-road to Plymouth and South Devon, and the High Street was grey with grime spewed out by traffic. All that has gone: the cars, lorries and coaches now follow the A38 to bypass the town, and are treated to a tempting, if fleeting, view of the back gardens and windows of some of the town houses. The town is sited on a long ridge, which ends

Exe estuary – avocet

Berry Pomeroy Castle
The ruins of Berry Pomeroy Castle surpass the wildly romantic images of *Boys' Own* magazine; they are sinister and fantastic, ivy-covered and dripping with undergrowth. The castle stands on a rocky limestone crag beside the steep-sided valley of the Gatcombe Brook, 2½ miles north-east of Totnes and is being restored.

Since the Norman Conquest the parish has been in the possession of only two families – the Pomeroys and the Seymours, some of whom, or their retainers, if the stories are true, have remained to haunt the battered walls. Folklore has made giants of the families and the knights who once roamed the wooded combes – one Sir Henry is said to have donned full armour and leapt, sounding a blast on his horn, on his blindfold charger over the cliff to his death, to avoid arrest.

The castle dates from the 14th century when the gatehouse and massive curtain wall were built; inside the quadrangle are the ruins of a great Tudor house, with a hall nearly 50ft long – in 1548 Edward Seymour, Duke of Somerset, purchased the castle and spent a fortune on the house, 'but never brought it to perfection'. In the 17th century, another Edward became Speaker of the House of Commons; he made his home at Maiden Bradley, Wiltshire, and Berry Pomeroy was abandoned; less than 100 years later it was falling into decay.

abruptly at the Rock, a great lump of limestone, once a popular picnic spot for outings from Exeter, overlooking the valley of the River Teign. Pixies' Cave, in the Rock, can be safely explored – prehistoric animal bones have been found in it.

The bishops of Exeter had a medieval palace at Chudleigh, and one of them, probably Bishop Stapeldon, founded a borough here. A reliable source of water was a major problem, on the limestone, until Bishop Lacey provided a town leat, in about 1430, which brought water from a spring on Haldon, about 7 miles away. In the 19th century, piped water was brought to the pump in the town square, by Harriet, Dowager Duchess of Morley – and the townsfolk even had a choice of hard or soft water. The main road brought trade, travellers and prosperity; there was a market and three fairs. St Martin's Church is mainly 14th century, but over-restored 100 years ago; the carved bench-ends are particularly interesting and there are numerous memorials – note that to Sir Pierce Courtenay, died 1552, in full armour. Next to the church, the old Grammar School is now a private house; it was founded in 1668 by John Pynsent.

On the south side of the ridge, at the bottom of Clifford Street, the old town mill has been imaginatively converted into the Wheel Craft Centre; visitors climb a steep staircase up through the floors of the mill to see craft workshops and crafts for sale alongside the mill machinery; there is also a restaurant.

TOTNES AND THE DART VALLEY
Totnes is a fascinating town, rich in history and yet vibrant with new ventures – there are several good shops and places to eat. About 8 miles upstream from Dartmouth, the town is on a hill rising from the west bank of the river up to the keep of the castle, on a mound at the top of the High Street.

The quayside is bustling with the activity of renovation; many of the old warehouses have been converted into new shops, restaurants and houses; but it is a working port too, with sizeable cargo boats from Finland and Sweden arriving regularly with timber, and cruises to and from Dartmouth. The first bridge over the river was built by the 13th century, when the Pomeroys founded a separate borough on the east bank – Bridgetown, now very much part of Totnes proper.

At the bottom of Fore Street, on the Plains, the monument is to William John Wills (1834–61), who was born at number 3, The Plains: the first man, with Burke, to cross the Australian continent. He perished of starvation at Cooper's Creek on the return journey; there are a handful of mementos in the town museum.

The main shopping street, Fore Street, leads up the hill towards the broad arch over the road at the East Gate; set in the pavement, the Brutus stone is where, according to legend, Brutus stood to survey the area before founding Totnes and the British race; opposite, Atherton Lane is adorned with flowers and cottages painted the colours of Neapolitan ice-cream. Under the arch a footpath follows the ramparts of the old town walls round to the medieval Guildhall, behind the church: it was built in 1553 on the foundations of the refectory of Totnes Priory. Totnes burghers have been elected to the office of mayor in the Council Chamber since the Middle Ages: there is a list of 624 of them.

The Parish and Priory Church of St Mary dates from the 15th century; its glory is the stone rood-screen of delicate tracery carved out of Beer stone and painted, and matched only by the one in Exeter Cathedral. Notice the corporation pews, cushioned in red velvet plush.

At the top of the High Street the pillared

William Wills

Between the bottom of the High Street and the bridge over the River Dart at Totnes, the area known as the Plains, stands an obelisk commemorating the short but heroic life of William Wills. He was born in the town on 5 January 1834, the son of the local surgeon. In 1852 William emigrated to Australia, and together with his father and younger brother panned for gold at Ballarat, Victoria.

With the gold rush ebbing, William took up surveying and in 1860 was appointed surveyor to the Royal Society of Melbourne's expedition to be the first to cross the Australian continent from south to north.

The expedition, led by Robert O'Hara Burke, was exceptionally well equipped; the waggon train of horses and camels set off on 21 August 1860. Possible competition from a rival team out of Adelaide, led by John Stuart, drove Burke to make good speed; having set up a supply depot at Cooper's Creek, Burke decided to take three men, William Wills, John King and Charles Grey, and make a quick dash for the north coast at the Gulf of Carpentaria. Against all odds they made it.

The return journey was a nightmare; Grey died on the way and they were desperately short of food. Incredibly they managed to stagger to Cooper's Creek, only to find their supply depot deserted.

Wills and Burke died; King was cared for by the aborigines until eventually a rescue party found him.

Steam Railways

Two sections of the old Great Western Railway in Devon have been reopened by private enterprise to offer nostalgic rides on lovingly restored steam trains.

The Dart Valley Railway winds along the unspoilt river valley between Totnes and Buckfastleigh, through woodland and the landscaped estates of Dartington Hall. At the Buckfastleigh end there is an impressive model railway layout, shop and café, plus a collection of carriages and engines and an old signal box with levers to pull, the delight of every schoolboy. Alongside the station is the Buckfast Butterfly Farm, a series of covered gardens with butterflies from many parts of the world.

The Torbay and Dartmouth Railway runs between Paignton and Kingswear with a connection to a boat trip up the River Dart and the ferry across the river to Dartmouth. The Paignton entrance is by the British Rail station; the coastal scenery alone makes the trip well worthwhile with views on a good day as far as Portland Bill.

Connections link up with the British Rail timetable for main line trains at Totnes and Paignton.

arcades, the Butterwalk and Poultry Walk, once sheltered the market stalls on the pavement's edge; the new Market Place features an Elizabethan costumed market every Tuesday in the summer.

The castle is a classic example of Norman 'motte and bailey' design; it dates from the 11th century. The motte rises some 50ft and is crowned by a small circular castellated keep. The views from the ramparts, over the rooftops of the town and beyond to the Dart valley, are superb.

Many of the town's buildings are 16th and 17th century, notably the Elizabethan House, now the Totnes Museum, where a number of internal features can be seen, including elaborate plaster ceilings and 16th-century fireplaces. One room in the museum is dedicated to Charles Babbage and his invention, the Occulting Light, the forerunner of modern computers. Around the town, slate-hanging, a characteristic local form of weather-proofing in the 18th and 19th centuries, has disguised several buildings of much earlier date.

The Dart Valley Railway runs steam trains from Totnes to Buckfastleigh, a picturesque route twisting through the wooded valley, and with a Steam and Leisure Park at the terminus; there are full-size exhibits and one of the largest model railway layouts in the country. The Totnes Motor Museum is situated in a converted cider warehouse at the Steamer Quay on the east bank of the Dart: it houses an excellent collection of vintage, sports and racing cars – many of them still driven by their owners, Richard and Trisha Pilkington. There is even an Amphicar, designed to travel on water.

Nearby **Bowden House**, about a mile south, presents a costumed welcome from hosts in 1740 Regency dress and guided tours with afternoon teas. It houses a large collection of vintage cameras, as well as antique furniture, weaponry and pictures in a beautifully restored interior. The Tudor house was built in 1510 by John Giles, reputedly the richest man in Devon; in 1704 the Queen Anne façade was added.

From Totnes take the A385 then A384 towards Buckfastleigh; about a mile from the town a lane to the right enters the grounds of the **Dartington Estate**. It is a narrow drive but flanked by specimen trees and views of the River Dart in the valley and the buildings of Dartington Hall; the road continues back to the A384. Here at Shinner's Bridge the Cider Press Centre, once the home of Dartington cider, has been converted to a craft centre with numerous workshops and retail shops. There are demonstrations and events, and a riverside trail.

Follow the Dart Valley on the A384 to **Buckfastleigh**, an attractive little town on the old main road between Exeter and Plymouth. The original settlement was at Buckfast, about a mile upriver; Buckfastleigh was 'the clearing at Buckfast', and was probably founded in the 13th century. Up 196 cobbled steps, on the north-east side of the town, the views from the church are breathtaking.

In the churchyard are the ruins of an old chantry chapel, and a strange mausoleum erected over the tomb of Richard Cabell, who died in 1677, to contain his unquiet spirit – he was thought to have been in league with the devil. Tales of fire-breathing black dogs howling round this tomb are thought to have been adapted by Conan Doyle when he was researching *The Hound of the Baskervilles*.

Now free of through traffic, the narrow streets of the town, packed tight with cottages and small houses, are a pleasure to explore: Fore Street is the oldest part of Buckfastleigh, with courts of cottages tucked in behind the street frontages. In Chapel Street a row of

Dartington Hall and Gardens

The creative restoration of Dartington Hall from a derelict farmyard to an exquisite garden was the brainchild of Leonard and Dorothy Elmhirst who purchased the estate in 1925 for an experiment in the reconstruction of rural life. In a beautiful setting on the River Dart, north of Totnes, the breadth of their concept is illustrated by the series of banners, woven by Elizabeth Peacock, hanging in the Great Hall, which represent symbolically the work of the estate: farming, forestry, gardening, masonry, education, the arts. The gardens are open to the public free of charge (donations invited); cobbled and paved paths, through neat lawns, lead into the restored Tiltyard, like an amphitheatre with high-stepped grassy banks; a reclining figure by Henry Moore watches from under a canopy of chestnut trees. There are borders, a camellia walk, azalea dell, and other sculptures, like the Little Donkey, to find amongst the plants.

The Great Hall was built in the 14th century by John Holland, Duke of Exeter, a half-brother to Richard II; when the Elmhirsts bought it, it was open to the sky and derelict. It now provides a magical venue for concerts, drama, conferences and other cultural activities; elsewhere there is a gallery and cinema.

Buckfast Abbey
The rebuilding of the abbey at Buckfast is one of the wonders of the 20th century; unbelievably, six monks, only one of them with any experience of masonry work, started work in January 1907 and completed the magnificent Abbey Church, now the centre piece of this living monastic community in 1937. The original monastery was founded here in 1018. At the dissolution, the monks were forced to leave, and gradually the buildings fell into disrepair.

It was not until the end of the 19th century that a small group of Benedictine monks from France, headed by Abbot Anscar Vonier, contemplated the idea of restoration. They based the new building on the foundations of the original church and followed the style of late-Norman Cistercian architecture; they squared and faced blocks of the local blue limestone for walls, and used mellow golden Ham Hill stone from Somerset for the window arches and quoins.

The church has a wonderful luminous quality from the light reflected by the pale stone. The crowning achievement is the great east window, in the Chapel of the Blessed Sacrament, the work of Father Charles, an acknowledged master craftsman in stained glass. Other monks have specialised in other ways: one is a recognised world authority on beekeeping, others farm, teach, paint and make the famous 'Buckfast Tonic Wine'.

woolworkers' cottages is distinguished by the wooden shutters along the top storey – these were once louvres that were opened or closed according to the weather to dry the cloth hanging up inside. Wool-processing was the major activity until only 50 years ago and woollen mills once lined the banks of the River Mardle. In the 16th century the place was heavily industrialised with at least seven woollen mills, a tannery and a paper mill, and quarries and mines nearby. The local limestone quarries provided good building stone, and supplied a number of limekilns to produce lime to enrich the poor acidic soils of Dartmoor. There are also a number of caves in the local limestone scenery: the William Pengelly Cave Studies Centre in Higher Kiln Quarry is used for scientific research and is the haunt of greater and lesser horseshoe and Natterer's bats. The Studies Centre and museum are open only when voluntary stewards are available. All the caves are dangerous: only enter with a guide.

The Dart Valley Railway runs from Buckfastleigh to Staverton and Totnes; the Steam and Leisure Park here at the station are worth visiting. There is also a Butterfly Farm.

North of Buckfastleigh a minor road is signposted to **Buckfast**, the site of the great Abbey church, an incredible feat of faith and hard work by a handful of untrained monks. Just inside the gatehouse, the little moorland-style Methodist church, white-washed and plain, looks incongruous, and the village of Buckfast, mostly out of sight, is dwarfed by its surroundings.

From Buckfast a dense network of high-banked lanes leads back towards Totnes through some of Devon's least known but most attractive villages: Broadhemston, Staverton and Littlehempston.

3 Plymouth, the Tamar Valley and South-West Devon

Lying between Dartmoor and the sea, with Cornwall to the west, this area is dominated by river valleys and estuaries with a coastline of cliffs, rough headlands and isolated coves. The Plym, Tavy, Yealm and Erme all rise on the moor but the Tamar, forming the boundary with Cornwall for most of its length, rises a few miles from the north coast and skirts the higher land in its meandering course south-eastwards to the sea at Plymouth.

Most of the valley is thick ancient woodland, of oak and beech, with surprisingly few settlements in it, the result of its frontier status between the Celtic and Saxon kingdoms that made it a precarious place to live. An Iron Age fort overlooks the river at Dunterton on the A384 about 8 miles north of Tavistock. At Plymouth the Tamar, Tavy and Plym all join and create the deep-water port that has been the starting point for some of the most famous and momentous voyages in history, both in war and peace; naval fleets and exploits of discovery and colonisation have all set sail from here and given rise to over forty 'Plymouths' throughout the world.

The region is also rich in mineral deposits; it has produced tin, silver, lead, copper and

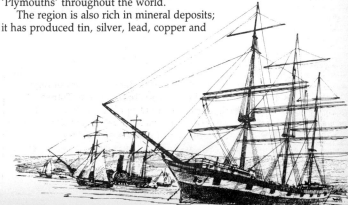

Plymouth

Population: 242,560

Market Days: Mon to Sat

Cashpoints: *Barclays* 19 Princess St, 48 Mutley Plain, 50 Cornwall St; *Lloyds* 165 Armada Way, 53 Mutley Plain, 8 Royal Parade, 3/5 Raleigh St; *Midland* 4 Old Town St, 65 Mutley Plain; *NatWest* 14 Old Town St, 61 Mutley Plain, 353 Southway Drive, 52 Royal Parade

Tourist Information: 12 The Barbican (summer only); Civic Centre, Royal Parade

Attractions: Armada Experience, City Museum and Art Gallery, Merchant's House Museum, Plymouth Dome, Prysten House*, Royal Citadel*, Smeaton Tower*

Arts: Barbican Theatre, Theatre Royal

Leisure: Fursdon Leisure Centre, Mayflower Centre, Seaton Barracks (Army, but may be opened to public)

Cinemas: Cannon Cinema, Drake Cinema

By Road: London 215 miles (A38, M5, M4), Exeter 44 miles (A38), Tavistock 15 miles (A386)

By Rail: 3hrs 15mins from London (London, Paddington to Penzance line). Direct services to Exeter, Penzance and Newton Abbot. Connections to Looe via Liskeard, Newquay via Par and Falmouth via Truro.

arsenic, most successfully near Tavistock, where, in the 1840s and 1850s the Devon Great Consul's mines were producing more than half the world's copper.

PLYMOUTH

By far the largest conurbation in Devon, **Plymouth** has existed as a single unit only since 1914, when the three towns of Devonport, Stonehouse and Plymouth were formally amalgamated, although physically they had been joined for many years. The original Saxon settlement was at Sutton – 'south town', which remained a small fishing village until the 13th century when trade with France began to flourish, and the name Plymouth began to be used. Even then it was overshadowed by ports like Dartmouth because although Plymouth has one of the finest deep-water harbours in Europe, it is open to the prevailing south-westerly winds, which would prevent ships from sailing for days on end. However, merchant, and increasingly, naval shipping began to bring prosperity to the town and by the 15th century Plymouth had become Devon's second city.

It was during the 16th century that Plymouth became nationally important as the starting point for voyages of discovery and colonisation, and perhaps most famously as a naval base in the war against Spain. Sir Francis Drake sailed from Plymouth to fight the Armada on 19th July 1588.

The choice of Plymouth as a naval headquarters was more to do with personalities than with natural assets; it was Drake's home port, and Sir Richard Hawkins, treasurer of the Navy from 1578–89, was a native of the town. The removal of the Spanish menace led to the town's decline, and in the 17th century it reverted to a trading and fishing centre; it was not until France's power became another threat that Plymouth again rose to importance. On this occasion, however, the navy decided to build a dockyard from scratch on the marshy land at the mouth of the Tamar to the west; it was given the unimaginative title of Dock, until 1824 when the residents petitioned for the more prestigious name of Devonport. Residential and commercial growth around the new dockyard during the wars with France temporarily eclipsed Plymouth in importance and population but with peace the situation reversed, and gradually, with the town of Stonehouse in between, the whole area merged.

The dockyard has dominated the town since the 19th century and its strategic value attracted the attention of the Third Reich during the Second World War and led to a series of horrific bombing raids on the city; 1,000 people killed and tens of thousands of buildings damaged or destroyed, the whole city centre wiped from the map. Ironically perhaps, the area to remain largely untouched was the site of the original settlement around Sutton harbour, the Barbican, which today has virtually all that remains of Plymouth's rich historical inheritance.

There are a number of car parks in the modern centre of the city, which consists of a rigid grid of streets divided into shopping, cultural and administrative blocks, partially pedestrianised. North is the City Museum and Art Gallery, which has Plymouth porcelain and Old Master drawings. South, on the sea front, at the eastern end of Royal Parade is St Andrew's Church, dedicated to the patron saint of fishermen and the largest parish church in the county. It is 13th-century with 14th- and 15th-century additions; the tower was constructed in 1461 and paid for by Thomas Yogge, a wealthy and pious local merchant. In 1941 it was completely gutted by fire, after being bombed, and has been painstakingly restored. Just behind the church, and miraculously surviving the air raids, is Prysten House, built by Yogge in 1498 round three sides of a galleried courtyard; originally covered in, it is now restored and open to the public.

Turn right from Prysten House – steps lead down to Merchant's House, a Tudor house remodelled in 1608 by William Parker from the profits of his raids on Spanish shipping. It has now an imaginative museum of Plymouth's history.

Continue down Finewell Street, left along Notte Street and then right into Southside Street, entering the heart of the Elizabethan town. On your right is Coates 'Blackfriars' Distillery; the famous Plymouth Gin has been made here since 1793, and the building contains some 19th-century stills. But the building dates from the 15th century and has served as a debtors' prison and Congregational meeting house.

Opposite is Blackfriars Ope (short for opening), and through here on Parade Quay are two of the old Custom Houses. On the near side is the oldest, dating from 1586; the more recent one, built in 1820, was designed by David Laing, whose London Custom House fell down after a couple of years use. The waterfront ahead is the original harbour of Plymouth, now busy with fishing and pleasure craft; under a canopy facing ranks of trawlers at the quayside, fishwives sit in yellow aprons, prising open scallops to cut out the rich orange and white flesh, and selling all varieties of fish from great plastic tubs.

Follow the harbour wall to the Barbican quay; thousands of vessels have sailed from here on voyages of adventure and discovery; some are commemorated by plaques; Drake's circumnavigation of the globe in 1577; the voyage of the Pilgrim Fathers in the *Mayflower* in 1620; the transport of convicts from the western gaols to join the First Fleet of prisoners bound for Botany Bay in 1787; the brave journeys of many thousands of free emigrants seeking a new life in the New Worlds of North America and Australia. In 1838, another plaque recalls the triumphant return of the Tolpuddle Martyrs.

Leading away from the quayside is New Street, containing most of the oldest buildings still standing; the Elizabethan House is sympathetically furnished with oak benches, settles and sideboards, and a fine 17th-century bed. Further along the waterfront is the Citadel, an imposing fortress of angular bastions, built under orders from Charles II who came to Plymouth twice to inspect the work. A new fort had been built just sixty years previously, but was demolished: it is thought that Charles wanted to impress the residents because they had been so staunch in their support of the Parliamentary cause during the Civil War, and so built this impregnable edifice to house his troops. It is now the base of 29 Commando Royal Artillery; official tours are available, revealing the 17th-century Governor's House, the fine baroque gateway and original armaments on the ramparts.

The road gradually climbs towards the large clifftop area, the Hoe. From Plymouth Hoe the expanse of the Sound can be appreciated, stretching from Penlee Point on the western side to Heybrook Bay in the east; the view is enhanced from the top of Smeaton's Tower, an old Eddystone Lighthouse re-erected here in 1882. The Hoe is dotted with memorials: Drake's statue, the Naval War Memorial, the Royal Marine Memorial and the National Armada Memorial. Here too the Plymouth Dome has audio-visual displays on city history.

In the Sound lies **Drake's Island**, rising to 96ft and covering 6 acres; it is an adventure centre. From 1550 to 1956 it was a military fortress; before that it had a chapel dedicated

Smeaton's Tower

Sir Francis Drake
Born near Tavistock in about 1541, Drake learned his sailing skills in the Medway in Kent, where his family moved when he was 15 to avoid religious persecution. In 1567 he began his career as a privateer, attacking the Catholic Spanish ships loaded with gold and treasures from America, culminating in a two-year trip that saw him return to Plymouth with ivory, spices, hides and wood from Brazil; gold, precious stones, silver, silk and velvet from Central America.

It was on this voyage that, in Panama, he saw the Pacific Ocean which was the inspiration to attempt a circumnavigation of the earth. He departed in December 1577 with four ships: his own Golden Hind was the only one left by the time they reached the Magellan Straits.

Sailing up the western coast of America they raided Spanish ports and ships, taking them completely by surprise, as no-one expected a sole English vessel. Heading across the Pacific they were out of sight of land for 60 days before reaching Indonesia. They returned to Plymouth in September 1580, becoming the first Englishmen to achieve the feat.

After his successful exploits defeating the Armada in 1588, there were fears that the Spanish might try again and on a voyage to thwart them he caught dysentry and died on 28th January 1596. He was buried at sea near Porto Bello, Panama.

to St Nicholas on the summit and was owned by the Plympton Priory. Known as St Nicholas Island, it received its present name when Drake was made governor in 1583. Beyond lies Plymouth breakwater, built between 1812–40. It is nearly a mile long and used about 4,500,000 tons of limestone, making the Sound safe from westerly gales; it has a lighthouse, first lit in 1844. Another lighthouse, visible on clear days, is the famous Eddystone Rock. Fourteen miles out to sea, the first lighthouse here was built in 1696; the present one was lit in 1882, and has become the model for subsequent lighthouses on similar reefs.

The old town of **Devonport** contains all the naval establishments and residences and is a generally dreary, grey mass of tenements and high walls that hide the dockyards, but there are some interesting sights amongst it all.

Leave the city centre westwards – along Royal Parade, across the roundabout and into Union Street. At the roundabout at the end, continue straight on into Cumberland Road across Stonehouse Bridge – no longer a bridge, the land to the right having been reclaimed. On the left is Stonehouse Creek, full of small fishing and pleasure craft and surrounded by boatyards. Turn first right into King's Road, and at the end left into Paradise Road. Park here and walk into the gardens across the road, keep to the left, and at the top of the hill is a splendid view of the dockyard stretching along the Tamar estuary: cranes, scaffolding and ships crowd along the water's edge in front of the huge workshops. The most striking buildings are the twin-towered factory at Keyham Steam Yard, first used in 1853, and consisting of foundries, machine shops, offices and storehouses; and the three massive frigate repair docks, opened in 1977, enabling work to be carried out in all weathers.

Continue along Paradise Road. At the end, turn left into Chapel Street then right into Ker

Street, where the line of characterless tenements suddenly ends in a unique collection of unusual buildings. The old Town Hall, built in 1821, was modelled on the Parthenon; next to it is a monumental column built in 1824 to celebrate the renaming of Dock to Devonport: it was to have had a statue of King George IV on the top, but the funds were never forthcoming. Back on the street, the Civil and Military Hospital, renamed the Oddfellows Hall, was built in the Egyptian style; it is now unfortunately very run down. This odd collection was all the work of the architect John Foulston, whose designs influenced the development of Plymouth during the 19th century in both the public and private sector.

Leave Plymouth westwards, following the signs to the A38, Exeter road, and at the large roundabout turn off to **Plympton**, the common name for two villages – Plympton St Mary in the north and Plympton St Maurice in the south, now merged.

An Augustinian priory was established in Plympton St Mary in 1121, and became the second largest in Devon; nothing remains of it now and although one of its properties was Plymouth it has since become little more than a suburb of the now thriving city. Plympton St Maurice has the substantial remains of a 12th-century castle, built by Richard de Redvers who was granted the manor by Henry I. Although the castle itself was destroyed, the earthworks dominate the centre of the village which grew up around it and prospered, leaving many fine old buildings: the Grammar School (where the father of Sir Joshua Reynolds was headmaster) was built in 1664; the Guildhall, dated 1688–96, is an interesting granite and slate construction and Plympton House, finished in 1720, has a fine Queen Anne front and its original gardens.

Leave Plympton southwards and cross the A38 leading to **Saltram House**, a magnificent

Sir Joshua Reynolds

Born in Plympton in 1723, the seventh son of the headmaster of Plympton Grammar School, Reynolds showed precocious talent; he used sailcloth and boat paint from the nearby Plymouth docks for his first paintings, but later studied in London and at 19 established himself as a portrait painter in Devonport.

One, Captain Keppel, took him on a voyage to the Mediterranean where he studied the Italian masters: his obsession with Classicism took hold and was to dominate his style. On his return to England he quickly established himself as the foremost portrait artist of the time, painting people of all levels of society from the king to paupers, producing as many as 184 pictures a year.

In 1769 he was knighted; four years later he was elected Mayor of Plympton, which he regarded as an even greater honour, and to commemorate it he painted a self-portrait for the Council Chamber which was hung between two 'old masters'. He pointed out to the ignorant members that they were in fact two of his early efforts. In later years he gradually went blind; he died in 1792.

Drake's Drum

Burgh Island

A 28-acre rocky island off the coast of South Devon near Bigbury-on-Sea, Burgh Island was purchased in the 1920s by Archibald Nettlefold, an eccentric millionaire who set about building a luxurious guest house as a place to entertain his business associates and friends. It recently changed hands and the house is being restored to its former art-deco glory by the new owners.

The island is connected to the mainland by a narrow causeway, covered at high tide, with fierce currents rendering it most inaccessible. Visitors have to travel by the sea tractor, and extraordinary machine designed and built in Newton Abbot, which ploughs through up to seven feet of water.

Among the famous visitors Nettlefold invited to Burgh Island were Noel Coward, the Duke of Windsor and Mrs Simpson, and Agatha Christie, who wrote several books whilst there: *Evil Under the Sun* is actually set on Burgh Island. More recent visitors have been Kirk Douglas and the Beatles.

Apart from the 'hotel', there is also a 14th-century inn, haunted by the ghost of a local smuggler, and at the top of the hill is the Huer's Hut, from which shoals of pilchards were spotted, and a hue and cry raised to prompt action.

George II mansion with original contents and housing a collection of paintings begun at the suggestion of Reynolds and including many of his portraits. Two rooms were designed by Robert Adam, and have superb decorated plasterwork and period furniture. The house is set in beautiful surroundings overlooking the Plym estuary. There was a Tudor mansion on the site, which was first registered as a manor in 1249; the present house was built at the beginning of the 18th century although altered and enlarged at least three times since then.

IVYBRIDGE

Returning to Plympton, join the A38 towards Exeter and, after about seven miles, there is a turning to the small market town of **Ivybridge**. Ivybridge is the fastest growing residential area in Devon, partly as a dormitory to Plymouth and partly in its own right, with industrial units springing up all round the periphery. The major redevelopment includes the South Dartmoor Leisure Centre, with indoor and outdoor swimming pools, a gymnasium, squash courts and coffee shop and bar. The provision of craft shops, riverside walks and play areas, and a new tourist information centre, will transform the town centre. This modern development, and the fact that little of any great age has survived, makes it rather characterless, but in every direction outside the town there is much to explore.

The main car park, at the centre of the new building work, is where to start an exploration. Leave over the new bridge across the Erme which leads to Fore Street, turn right and, by the bridge, left into Erme Road. At the end is the old bridge over the river, built to take the increased traffic created by the development of Plymouth as a trade centre. A bridge was first recorded here in 1280. Continue along the road with the river on your right; across the river the large, mostly Victorian, factory is Stowford

Mill, the only remaining one of two paper mills that thrived in the town. By the entrance to the mill a path enters the woods, but the way is often very muddy so the road is recommended. Turn right into Station Road and immediately the great railway viaduct comes into view, towering over the road and river. Just past the viaduct are the towers of the original railway designed by Brunel in 1848: the upper part was of wood, demolished when the new one was constructed to take the doubled South Devon Line of the Great Western Railway in 1893. A path entering the wood here leads to a delightful riverside walk.

Leave Ivybridge south over the A38, along the B3211 to Ermington, turn right onto the B3210, and then left onto the A379 to **Modbury**, set in a steep dip with attractive streets rising on all sides.

Originating as a Saxon settlement, Modbury developed into an important market town until the last century when the growing importance of the railway left it out on a limb. The annual St George's Fair was abandoned in the 1880s, although its rebirth in 1971 shows the town spirit that still survives. The architecture is mostly 18th- and 19th-century. The church is largely 14th-century with a medieval spire, unusual for Devon. It is well maintained and cared for; the northern doorway is known as Prior's Doorway because it faces the site of an old Priory.

Continuing through Modbury on the A379 turn left onto the B3392 to **Bigbury-on-Sea**, a scattered village with a great deal of modern tourist development, but with a superb beach and the added attraction of Burgh Island, accessible only at low tide, either by foot or 'taxi', with a 13th-century inn and good views. A chapel existed on the island, dedicated to St Michael, but nothing of it now remains.

Returning to the A379 pass through Modbury and after about 4 miles turn left to

Holbeton, a substantial village with a striking monument to the Hele family in the spacious church: a three-tiered series of effigies. At the top is Thomas Hele of Exeter and family, beneath him is his son, another Thomas, and the figure in armour at the bottom is the grandson, Sir Thomas Hele of Flete.

Continue through the village to **Mothercombe**, standing at the mouth of the Erme in outstanding scenery both inland up the estuary and along the rocky coast. From Mothercombe the coastal road leads to **Noss Mayo** and **Newton Ferrers**, facing each other across a tributary of the Yealm estuary. The old Noss Mayo church is now a romantic ruin isolated on the cliffs about a mile and a half south-east of the village near Stoke Point and walks along this part of the coast are spectacular, with great sheets of slate rising out of the sea and isolated coves to explore.

Turning inland along the B3186 leads to **Yealmpton** on the A379. A fairly nondescript village set in attractive woodland, its claim to fame is that it was the home of Old Mother Hubbard, the housekeeper at nearby Kitley where the rhyme was written by Sarah Martin in 1805.

One mile east of the village is the National Shire Horse Centre with many other animals other than horses, craft exhibitions and displays, all in some fine old farm buildings.

Continuing along the A379 towards Plymouth turn left to **Wembury**, set on a piece of wild, windswept coast. The church stands alone on the cliff, probably to act as a landmark for mariners, and its striking 14th-century tower stands dramatically, silhouetted against the sky.

The Mew Stone, a mile offshore, was once inhabited but is now the home of fulmars and kittiwakes; on the beach the National Trust has restored an old mill which serves refreshments during the summer months. Walking either

Tavistock Court Gate

east or west from here is easy along the clifftops with superb views of Plymouth Sound and the Yealm estuary.

TAVISTOCK

Ten miles north of Plymouth on the River Tavy, **Tavistock** is the only market town of any size in this part of Devon. Its history has two distinct phases created by its two owners: Tavistock Abbey from the 10th to the 16th century and, after the dissolution of the monasteries, the Russells: earls, and later dukes, of Bedford. There is evidence of a small Saxon settlement, but it was not until 974, with the founding of a Benedictine abbey, that any impetus was given to the town. The abbey was destroyed by invading Danes after only 16 years of existence, but it was rebuilt and grew to become the wealthiest in the south-west; in 1105 permission to hold a Friday market was granted, and it continues to this day; a fair was added in 1116.

From the 12th century tin-mining led to even greater prosperity: Tavistock became one of the three stannary towns in Devon, where tin was officially weighed, stamped and sold. Tin-mining declined in the 17th century, but a growing wool trade took its place and prevented any decline, and when in turn the new mills in the north of England took this trade, copper was discovered and Tavistock thrived as it had never done before. The population of the town trebled in the first half of the 19th century.

The Russells owned not only the town but also the land where the copper was found and the great wealth created was used by Francis Russell to completely rebuild and restyle the centre of the town, much of it in an unusual local stone of greenish hue; his statue now surveys the spacious Victorian streets and Gothic façades from in front of the guild-hall. By the beginning of the present century the

Pilgrim Fathers
A plaque at Bayards Cove, Dartmouth, marks the spot where the *Mayflower* and *Speedwell*, carrying the Pilgrim Fathers, put in for repairs in 1620 on their way from Southampton to start a new life in the New World free from religious persecution.

Despite the repairs, the *Speedwell* was found to be unseaworthy, and a further stop was made at Plymouth. Here the *Speedwell* was abandoned; but the emigrants were warmly welcomed by the people of Plymouth; they were treated to a farewell service in St Andrew's Church, and dinner in a house which still survives in the Barbican. On 15 August 1620, the *Mayflower* alone set off on the final leg of her journey across the Atlantic – again, a plaque marks the spot in the Barbican.

They reached America in November, with the loss of only one life on board and named their new home 'New Plymouth'. The pilgrims struggled through their first winter, desperately short of food and suffering from terrible cold with inadequate shelters; half of them perished. The survivors created the foundations of a society that was to draw increasing numbers of emigrants from Europe searching for freedom and opportunity.

Today's descendants of those *Mayflower* pilgrims form the membership of one of North America's most exclusive clubs.

Wassailing

To ensure a good crop of apples for cidermaking the following season the orchards of the West Country were once wassailed in a traditional ceremony that dates back to Saxon times:

Old Apple Tree, Old Apple Tree
We wassail thee and hope that thou wilt bear
hat fulls
cap fulls
three bushel bags full,
* and a little heap under the stairs.*

The word Wassail is a corruption of two Saxon words meaning 'good health'; so the tradition is a toast to the orchard.

Twelfth Night, 5th January, was the most common night for the event, although New Year's Eve and even Christmas Eve were the dates chosen in some areas. Participants assembled under the oldest or largest tree in the orchard, singing and then firing off guns or beating the trunk with sticks to scare off any evil spirits that might be lurking. Naturally, plenty of cider was drunk.

copper mines were exhausted and Tavistock returned to its more traditional role as a market centre for the western side of Dartmoor.

Bedford Square, the centre of the town, has the parish church of St Eustace on the western side. A mainly 15th-century building it contains two fine monuments: one to Sir John Glanville, a prominent attorney and judge, lying on his side with a hand on a skull; and the other to Sir John Fitz and his wife. The south side of the churchyard contains one of the few remaining parts of the once magnificent abbey, a corner of the cloister arcade; across the square is the abbey gateway, built in the 12th century and remodelled in the 15th; towards the bridge is the misericord (dining hall), now a Unitarian chapel.

Otherwise, the only remaining part is the abbey wall and Still Tower, reached by turning right down a small path before the bridge over the river. On the eastern side of the square are the main public buildings created by the Duke of Bedford in the 1850s and 60s: the town hall, guild-hall and pannier market. Duke Street and Plymouth Road, leading off the square to the north and south, also contain many pleasant private houses and shops from the same period.

Leave Tavistock on the Plymouth Road: at the end is the original Drake's Statue, the more famous one on Plymouth Hoe being a replica. Drake was born 1 mile south of Tavistock at Crowndale Farm which has since been demolished. Follow the signs to **Morwellham Quay**, 4 miles away, where the remains of the industrial prosperity of Tavistock can be seen in the beautiful setting of the Tamar Valley. Morwellham was the nearest point to Tavistock which sea-going ships could navigate and when the huge copper deposits were discovered at Blanchdown 5 miles to the north major industrial development began: a 4-mile canal was built from the centre of Tavistock,

including a 2-mile tunnel through Morwell
Down, and from high above the river an
inclined railway brought the ore down to the
quayside. The exhaustion of the mines led to
the decline of the area and it gradually
disintegrated into rusting heaps and bramble-
covered waste. In 1970 a charitable trust was
established to restore the site.

Restoration has been achieved with great
skill and sensitivity to the natural environment
as well as the industrial heritage, creating a
number of displays with a sense of living
history. Cottages have been faithfully restored,
complete with a pig in the yard, and friendly
staff in 1860s costume recreate the life at the
time and demonstrate the traditional crafts of
the smith and the cooper in their refurbished
workshops. A working Victorian farm is
complete with shire horses, which provide the
power for carriage rides along the Duke of
Bedford's drive, and a miniature railway carries
visitors deep underground into a copper mine
last worked in 1868. There are also three
museums portraying the various aspects of life
in the boom years, an introductory slide show
and walks through woodland along the course
of the canal and railway.

Morwellham

Leaving Morwellham, turn right at the top
of the hill to **Bere Alston** and **Bere Ferrers**. The
villages occupy a tongue of land between the
Tamar and the Tavy, Bere coming from the
Welsh 'ber' meaning spit or point. Bere Alston
is now a small town, having grown because of
the silver-lead workings that have been
intermittently productive since the 13th
century. Bere Ferrers is the older, although
now smaller, settlement right on the Tavy in a
beautiful setting, with a fine 14th- and 15th-
century church, St Andrews. Sir William de
Ferrers established a collegiate church here in
about 1330, and much of the work remains: the
east window has some of the oldest glass in
Devon; there is a richly-carved Norman

font and 16th-century pew ends and book rests.

Leave the village west by the bridge over the railway and this road returns to Bere Alston along the heavily wooded valley of the Tamar, and past some derelict quays that transported the ore from the local mines. From the town travel east to **Buckland Monachorum**, containing many fine old buildings as well as some particularly unattractive modern ones; the church is an unaltered 15th- and early 16th-century construction with a fine lofty interior and monuments to the Drake family. The Garden House has an 8-acre garden and sheltered walled garden of interest throughout the year. One mile south of the village is the home of Sir Francis Drake, **Buckland Abbey**, originally a Cistercian Abbey, converted to residential use and now a naval and folk museum.

Founded in 1273 by Amicia, Countess of Devon, it was the most westerly Cistercian abbey in the country and thrived on the produce of expansive estates until the dissolution of the monasteries in 1539, when it was sold to the Grenville family. They demolished many buildings and converted the abbey church into a fine dwelling, with oak panelling and decorated plasterwork. Sir Francis Drake moved to Buckland in 1582, the year he became Mayor of Plymouth; it was his home until his death at sea in 1596, although there is little evidence of his occupation. The Abbey remained in the Drake family until 1946, when a local landowner bought it and later presented it to the National Trust.

The exhibitions of the varying life of the site are fascinating and contain many interesting relics, the most famous being Drake's drum, an object endowed with magical properties and said to sound a warning of impending danger to England's shores. The buildings themselves are also impressive, especially the 14th-century

Devon Red cow

tithe barn, larger than the church itself and a clear monument to the prosperity of the monastery in its heyday.

From the Abbey head towards Yelverton on the main A386 between Plymouth and Tavistock; turn onto the B3212 towards Princetown and then right to **Sheepstor**, a tiny village that took its name from the tor that overlooks it. Nearby **Burrator Reservoir**, covering 150 acres of the Meavy valley, was originally constructed in 1891 to serve Plymouth; it was almost doubled in size to over a thousand million gallons in 1928. An annual ceremony held at the reservoir is the 'Fishinge Feaste', where a toast is drunk to Sir Francis Drake who first brought water from the moor to supply Plymouth, with the words 'May the descendants of him who brought us waters never want wine.'

About five miles south of Sheepstor is the **Goodameavy Estate**, 400 acres of steep woodland overlooking the Plym and Meavy valleys, including the Dewerstone, a massive granite outcrop, popular with climbers, now owned by the National Trust. There are three well marked walks.

North from Sheepstor cross the B3212 through Walkhampton and down the narrow lanes to **Peter Tavy**: from here there are numerous interesting walks. The surrounding moor is rich in prehistoric and Iron Age remains, although a good map is needed to find them and care must be taken to avoid the times when the army uses the area as a firing range. Just across the river is **Mary Tavy**, these two villages taking their names from the church dedication. Just north of the village on the A386 is Wheal Betsy, the remains of a Cornish Beam engine house preserved by the National Trust; it was once the site of lead, zinc, silver, copper and arsenic mining.

Barnstaple

Population: 24,878

Early Closing: Wed

Market Days: Tue, Fri

Cashpoints: *Barclays* 38 Boutport St; *Lloyds* 17 Cross St; *Midland* 10 High St; *NatWest* 41 High St

Tourist Information: North Devon Library, Tuly St

Attractions: C H Brannan Ltd Pottery, Marwood Hill Gardens, Museum of North Devon, St Anne's Chapel and Old Grammar School Museum*

Leisure: Leisure Centre

By Road: London 216 miles (A361, M5, M4), Exeter 40 miles (A377)

By Rail: 1hr 10mins from Exeter (on a branch of the London, Paddington to Penzance line). Direct service to Exeter. Connections to Exmouth, Plymouth, Teignmouth and Torquay via Exeter

Valley of Rocks

4 North-East Devon

From the sweeping sand and dunes of the west coast at Braunton, and from the cosy market towns of Chulmleigh, South Molton and Bampton, to the rugged furze-topped hills of Exmoor, north-east Devon is a roller-coaster landscape, best seen on the north coast at Girt Down and Hangman Point.

To the south the Carboniferous Culm Measures have yielded a soft sooty coal, known as culm, and here it forms a low plateau sliced by rivers and streams. Further north the old red sandstone has been uplifted and carved even more dramatically, creating chasms of dense woodland in contrast to the sparse vegetation on the high hill tops. Deeply cutting rivers have etched steep-sided valleys, notorious to drivers following the coastal holiday routes.

Exmoor National Park is cut in two by the county boundary between Devon and Somerset: just about one third of the park falls within Devon, but on this side of the border there are a number of fascinating places to visit, each characteristic in one way or another of the whole moor. The coastline is magnificent and the North Devon Coast path meets with that of Somerset to link spectacular cliffs, rocky bays and wooded combes.

BARNSTAPLE

Reputed to be one of the oldest towns in Devon, **Barnstaple** was well established by 1086 at the time of the Domesday survey, and from 978 to 1100 even minted its own coins. The name is derived from old English, meaning Bearda's *stapol* or post. Bearda is thought to be a chief amongst the earlier settlers on the site. Barnstaple's advantage as a progressive port and centre for trading and business was largely due to its position on the River Taw, at the lowest crossing point, and the highest navigable stretch of water. It became a focal point for industries – especially woollen manufacture, although this fell into decline in the late 18th century, but the port remained active and continued as a flourishing import centre in the 19th century, with goods from the Baltic, France, Spain and North America. Barnstaple naturally developed as the main administrative centre for North Devon.

Park in the cattle market car-park next to the new library and tourist information office; behind this is the distinctive shape of the Castle Mound, 60ft high. The Mound is the 'motte' of a 'motte and bailey' castle, with the Castle Green occupying the site of the bailey. The exact date is unknown, although it is believed to have been built shortly after 1066 by the Normans to give them control over the town. No buildings remain from this period; it is known that the motte had a circular stone tower, surrounded by a stone wall and a deep moat fed by the nearby river. The top of the castle provided an excellent vantage point for viewing the town and the river.

Across Tuly Street from the library, facing the cattle market, is a fine example of early 20th-century commercial architecture, strongly classical in style, with sculpted relief pediments and entablature, dated 1903. With the cattle market to the right, walk down Tuly Street and turn up Holland Walk to the High Street;

Barnstaple

it is largely pedestrianised and creates an impression of a typical busy market town, with pleasing 19th-century façades reflecting the town's prosperity, although many have been subjected to modernisation as large supermarket chains have gained control.

Turn right up the High Street. Notice the Three Tuns Tavern on the right, a rare remaining example of 15th-century architecture, built in 1450, with fine oak panelling and beamed ceilings. Turn left from here into the Pannier Market, a magnificent structure designed by the local architect R D Gould in 1855. Gould was responsible for the major redevelopment of the town in the mid-19th century, and many projects bear his mark. The market epitomises the very best in contemporary engineering techniques, with its fine timber and iron roof construction, more reminiscent of a railway station than a market hall, covering 45,000 square feet; on Tuesdays and Fridays it is packed with stall holders and prospective purchasers jostling for bargains.

Leave the market through the arched brick openings on the right into Butchers Row, built at the same time as the market to cater for the town's 33 butchers in small individual booths. The overhanging roof is supported by Bath stone pilasters and wrought-iron brackets. From Butchers Row a small alley leads to the churchyard, a delightfully secluded grassy area with the main walk flanked by shady lime trees. St Peter's church to the right is probably of pre-Norman foundation; the present building dates back to 1107, but is mainly 14th-century. Sadly, it was heavily restored in the 19th century, by Sir Gilbert Scott, leaving it dark and gloomy and of little interest, save for its monuments to 17th-century merchants, and magnificent leaded spire, dated 1636. The odd twisting of the spire has been attributed to a lightning strike of 1810, but is more likely to be the result of continual exposure to the sun.

Behind the church in Paternoster Row is
14th-century St Anne's Chapel, once a school;
it now houses a small local history museum.
Pass along narrow Church Lane, where on the
left are the almshouses founded by Thomas
Horwood in the mid-17th century, clustered
around a delightful enclosed courtyard. Next
door is the school building erected in 1659 by
his wife, Alice, 'for 20 poor maids', which is
now a coffee house. Back on the High Street
turn left; at the far end, next to the Royal and
Fortescue Hotel, are the present offices of the
Woolwich Building Society. Inside is one of the
finest plaster ceilings in Devon, moulded and
barrel-vaulted, dated 1620, and representative
of the county's tradition of urban plasterwork,
most notable in Barnstaple and Totnes.

The road opens out into the Square,
designed in 1723, although much influenced in
the 19th century by Gould, who designed the
Albert Memorial Clock in the centre in 1862.
Across the road is the North Devon
Athenaeum, built in about 1870, and presented
to the town by William Rock, a local
benefactor, in 1887; he was also responsible for
the Rock Park, a stretch of gardens alongside
the River walk to the south of the bridge.

Pottery, Barnstaple

The bridge is perhaps Barnstaple's most
striking feature. The first bridge was built in
the 13th century, but the present structure
dates from the 15th century. It is 700ft long,
with 16 arches, and has been the subject of
endless widening and restoration, although the
original structure is still clearly visible from the
pedestrian underpass. A pleasant walk has
been created alongside the river.

Head north up the quayside; it was from
here, in 1588, that the town responded to the
national alert of the Spanish Armada, and
promptly despatched five ships to join Francis
Drake at Plymouth. Just past the Bus Station
on the right, is Queen Anne's Walk, an
elaborate colonnade surmounted by a statue of

Queen Anne, built in 1709 as a merchants' exchange. It has been the subject of extensive recent renovation along with a general scheme to improve the ambience of the river frontage. The majestic Queen, clutching her orb and sceptre, stands above the 'Tome' stone – a 17th-century stone pillar which stood on the quay, where bargains were struck by the merchants – once money had passed over the stone any contract was binding.

Leave the riverside walk beyond the old Town Railway Station, now a restaurant, and cross North Walk to return to Castle Green.

The village of **Braunton**, west of Barnstaple on the A361, consists largely of sprawling modern housing estates, the older part being on the hillside east of the main road. Here there are some traditional North Devon farmhouses, with their characteristic massive stone chimneys on the street, and the church, dedicated to St Brannock, a Welsh missionary-saint of the 6th century. He founded a chapel, on the spot, revealed to him in a dream, where he found a sow and a litter of pigs; the present church, probably on the same site, is largely 13th-century – one of the carved roof-bosses shows a sow and her farrow. The carved bench ends, 16th- and 17th-century, are amongst the finest in the country.

South-west of the village are Braunton Burrows, a large area of vegetation and sand dunes forming the end of the estuary of the Torridge and Taw; take the B3231 towards Croyde, and turn left down the lane where the houses end; to the car park about 1½ miles away. This lane runs alongside Braunton Great Field, a rare relic of medieval open-field cultivation: 350 acres divided into strips by grass balks, a foot wide; within living memory, it has been farmed by some 85 farmers, although now less than a dozen use the land.

A walk across **Braunton Burrows** reveals a wild and natural moonscape of mountainous

sand dunes, 4 miles long and over 1 mile wide.
The wind-blown sand has been captured and
held by the roots and stems of the marram
grasses, and is a paradise for botanists. There
are more than four hundred species of
flowering plants, scented carpets of colour –
purple thyme, yellow birds foot trefoil, deep-
blue vipers bugloss – interlaced with vivid
yellow stonecrop and fragile purple orchids.
Fox, hedgehog, mole, mink, shrew and vole
creep into holes hidden in the undergrowth
and are hard to spot, but rabbits, warblers and
seabirds are everywhere and on hot summer
days the cushioned hollows of the dunes
provide popular niches for sun-worshipping
humans.

*Braunton Burrows –
marsh helleborine*

The B3231 continues through **Saunton**,
which is a small village noted for
its fine golf course. There is also a beach
here. After Saunton, the road goes on to
Croyde. As it climbs, there are magnificent
views back towards Braunton Burrows and
north to Croyde Bay and Baggy Point; lay-bys
provide stopping points to take in the scene at
leisure. The road drops down into Croyde, a
popular holiday village with many guest-
houses and nearby camping and caravan sites.
The small beach lies across sand dunes, and to
the north is Baggy Point; to the south-west is
Hartland Point, to the north, Morte Point and
Morte Bay, with the best sandy beach in north
Devon.

To reach **Morte Bay** from Croyde, turn left
in the middle of the village, signposted to
Putsborough; a steep, narrow lane leads up
over the headland past the turning to the
village to a car-park. There is a hotel, a beach
shop, and a few holiday homes, but little else,
so it has not developed into a large tourist
attraction, despite having a superb stretch of
sand. Holidaymakers tend to congregate at the
north end of the bay, at Woolacombe, where
there are more facilities.

The Longhouse
The design of the traditional Devon farmhouse remained basically the same for at least 500 years; the earliest examples are those at the abandoned medieval village on Houndtor which show the basic plan that was adapted through the ages. These houses consist of a long rectangle cut across the middle by a passage which opens to the outside at both ends, and has one room on either side. They were often built on a slope; the upper room, or 'hall', was the room for humans; the lower for animals, the slope aiding essential drainage. The hall was sometimes sub-divided to provide separate cooking and living areas, with a chimneyless hearth on the end wall.

As the county became more affluent, especially during the 17th century, a desire to further divide, or extend, this basic plan was introduced, to provide separate rooms for the various functions of the household.

Animals were removed to out-buildings and new rooms were built on to extend the length of the longhouse, although this sometimes made access difficult. A single-storey lean-to or second floors were alternative options.

To reach **Woolacombe** from Croyde continue through the village on the B3231 and join the B3343 at Turnpike Cross: this is a narrow, twisting lane, with attractive cottages tight to the road. The A361 from Barnstaple is an easier road, following a valley for most of the way; then turn left on to the B3343 at Mullacott Cross. Both routes are well signposted. Woolacombe was developed from the 1820s by the Chichesters and Fortesques (of Arlington Court), who owned most of the land; the handful of original cottages and a farm gave way to rest homes, villas and hotels; up the combe a rash of caravan and camping sites now covers the grassy slopes.

The moorland around, now owned by the National Trust, and the superb coastline are easily accessible and offer lovely walks, either steeply up the narrow combes, or along the sweeping curve of the bay.

From Woolacombe follow the coastal road to **Mortehoe**, sheltering just under the brow of the ridge that forms Morte Point; the little village is scarcely protected from the fierce westerlies. Its character is derived from the grey Morte slates from which it is built; the church, the pub and farm emerge from the landscape with almost no transition from stone outcrop to buttressed walls. The striking cliff scenery with razor edges and glistening surfaces leads out to the treacherous Morte Stone, on which no less than five ships foundered in the winter of 1852.

Through the sun-bleached timbers of the lych gate, the church, St Mary's, is largely unrestored; the first chapel, almost certainly on this site, was founded by Sir William de Tracy as a penance for his involvement in the murder of Thomas à Becket. The present church is 13th-century, with later additions: its greatest treasures are the carved bench ends, 16th-century, depicting sea monsters, coats of arms, portraits and the instruments of the Passion.

EXMOOR

The land at the north-eastern edge of Devon rises abruptly from gently rolling farmland, forming the edge of Exmoor – a high plateau, criss-crossed by many tiny streams and deeply cut river valleys, bounded at the north by steep cliffs dropping into the Bristol Channel. Most of the high moor is in Somerset, the Devon side consisting of wooded valleys and isolated farms, with spectacular cliffs as the main attraction. The county boundary in the north follows Badgworthy Water, running the length of the Doone Valley, the home of the evil Doones in R D Blackmore's *Lorna Doone*, which although a work of fiction has many real connections with the area. The Doones terrorised Exmoor, from their stronghold in Lank Coombe where the tiny stream is towered over by 300ft hills. At the head of the valley is Doone Gate, the main approach to the enclave, marked by a large stone rather than a gate.

The county boundary follows a ridge southwards, marked by such evocative names as Breakneck Hole, Edgerley Stone, Wood Barrow and Setta Barrow, until it reaches another river forming the southern boundary: Dane's Brook, which joins the River Barle near Dulverton.

Exmoor is made up of layers of hard sedimentary rocks: sandstones, slates and limestones; the principal vegetation is heather, gorse and purple moor grass or 'flying bent', so called because in autumn the dry grasses snap in the wind and blow across the moor. The valleys are heavily wooded; there are ancient oaks, but often ranks of Forestry Commission conifers dominate. The varied habitats support a wealth of wildlife, the most famous being Exmoor ponies, thought to be the ancestors of the wild horses of Europe, and red deer; both animals have roamed the moor for thousands of years, since long before the arrival of man. Barrows, stone circles and

Red Deer

The largest of Britain's wild animals, the red deer, is indigenous to Exmoor. Persistent hunting and gradual loss of habitat, as the moorland has been engulfed by agriculture, have reduced their range, but now strict management ensures the continuation of the species.

Small herds can often be glimpsed from the road, as these timid creatures have become more accustomed to traffic than to walkers, who rarely encounter deer at close quarters.

They are most visible in October and November, the rutting season, when the males roar their claims across the valleys in competition, to establish territory and form small herds with between five and ten breeding hinds. The young calves are born in June, and stay with the hinds for at least a year.

The stag's antlers are renewed each year until, at five, they have the full complement, although they can add more over the years if old ones are damaged. The average life-expectancy of a red deer is about fifteen years.

Exmoor – red deer

standing stones cover the moor, dating from the Beaker and Bronze Ages, the earliest evidence of human habitation.

The poor soil and inclement weather conditions mean that the moor has been mainly used for hunting. William the Conqueror proclaimed Exmoor a Royal Forest for that purpose, and protected it with draconian laws against any encroachment or poaching. In 1508, Henry VII leased the area to a Warden for £46 per annum and this led to greater agricultural use because farming was the only way for the Warden to increase his income: up to 30,000 sheep were grazed, with a smaller number of cattle. The heather, gorse and rushes also provided income, being used for kindling, stable litter, brushes and floor coverings.

In the 19th century the Knight family bought the forest outright and tried to develop its resources even more, enclosing large areas of land and encouraging prospecting for minerals, neither of which was as successful as they had hoped. In the present century the National Trust has gradually acquired land, and in 1954 a National Park was created of 170,000 acres, although nearly 150,000 are still privately owned: this should be considered when exploring the area, by respecting the land and those who make their living from it.

Inland, about 3 miles east of Lynton on the A39, is **Watersmeet**, where the Farley and Hoaroak Water join the River Lyn. Walks along the valleys reveal stunning hanging oaks, and Watersmeet House, a fishing lodge built in 1832, offers refreshments during the summer months.

Just outside the National Park, about 7 miles north of Barnstaple on the A39, is **Arlington Court**, part of a 2,780-acre estate bequeathed to the National Trust in 1949 by Miss Rosalie Chichester. Her house, built in 1822, contains many small *objets d'art*: pewter,

shells and model ships as well as furniture and
costumes from the 19th century, but it is the
collection of carriages and horsedrawn vehicles
that provide the greatest attraction and rides
are available.

Around the house is a landscaped park,
grazed by Shetland ponies and Jacob's sheep;
and a Victorian garden and conservatory,
which leads to a wooded valley and lake. A
path can be seen from the front of the house
leading out across the park; an obelisk off to
the left bears the inscription: 'On this spot a
bonfire was lit to commemorate the Jubilee of
Queen Victoria, June 21 1887.' Follow the path
and turn right to a hide by the lake. The two
massive stone piers that are visible either side
of the lake were built by Sir John Chichester in
the 19th century to take a bridge, but it was
never completed; there is a heronry behind the
pier to the west. Returning back along the lake
the path crosses the dam and into the woods.

ILFRACOMBE

The town of **Ilfracombe** rises in tiers of
terraced houses and grand hotels, behind the
busy harbour that was its heart long before the
arrival of holidaymakers to crowd the narrow
streets and stroll along the promenades. As
early as the 14th century it was an important
port, sending more ships and men to fight the
French under Edward III in 1346 than
Merseyside and, although gradually declining
over the next few centuries, as Barnstaple and
Bideford prospered, it still retained its herring
fleet.

In the last century, as the popularity of
seaside resorts grew, Ilfracombe again
flourished and the town is now dominated by
the Victorian villas, guest houses and hotels
built during that period; the hotel names
conjure up an air of affluent gentility –
Collingwood, Raffles, Grosvenor, Grand.

Ilfracombe remains a traditional resort,

Ilfracombe

Population: 10,424

Early Closing: Thu

Market Day: Sat

Cashpoints: *Midland* 150 High St

Tourist Information: The Promenade

Attractions: Chambercombe Manor*, Hele Mill*, Ilfracombe Museum, Watermouth Castle*

Arts: Pavilion Theatre

Leisure: Larkstone Sports Ground – Pitch and Putt Golf, Swimming Pool

Cinema: Pendle Stairway

By Road: London 229 miles (A361, M5, M4), Barnstaple 14 miles (A361)

By Rail: The nearest station is at Barnstaple, which is 1hr 10mins from Exeter

though modernised, the sounds of amusement arcades are dominated by seagulls screeching, and the rolling surf; the smell of the sea is stronger than that of candy floss.

The mixture of ancient and more modern development is exemplified at the harbour: it is still packed with vessels – pleasure craft and steamers ready to make trips along the coast, or to Lundy. Lantern Hill rises above the quayside; here a light from St Nicholas's Chapel, on the summit, was used for centuries to guide sailors along the treacherous coast. The old quay has been extended by a wooden promenade-pier, completed in 1873, to accommodate the increasing number and size of steamers transporting holidaymakers to and from the town. Across the harbour, rising almost vertically from the sea, is Hillsborough, a pleasant parkland; it can be reached by following the edge of the harbour and ascended by a number of paths, giving views to Wales, 20 miles away. Below is Hele Bay and the sheltered hamlet of Hele. There is also a panoramic view of the town and the Torrs beyond. Along the old pier the Lifeboat House, opened in 1828, welcomes visitors, the boots and waterproofs strung up like washing from the roof.

Continuing into town, to the right along Capstone Terrace is another steep headland, Capstone Hill, with an impressive Victorian promenade cut into the hillside. Further along the main coastal road, on the right just past the putting green, is the Ilfracombe Museum, a charitable enterprise, packed with diverse memorabilia of the town's past and exotic connections, gifts of retired colonials.

Turn right into Runnacleave Road: an austere Georgian-style building marks the entrance to one of the most fascinating and eccentric 19th-century developments of the town – the Tunnels Beaches, created in the 1830s. Passageways were hacked through the

rock to a bay and, by a combination of natural
rock formation and man-made walls, when the
tide receded, bathing-pools of sea water were
left behind. Initially bathing was segregated:
'the Westward part is allotted to Gentlemen,
while the Eastward is by custom left to the
Ladies'; not until 1905 was mixed bathing
allowed. The gentlemen's pool has been
eroded by sea and weather, but through the
second tunnel the ladies' pool remains, and is
still used – but today by both sexes.

Further along Runnacleave Road, any of the
right-hand turns lead to the Torrs Walk; zig-
zag paths cut through the wild undergrowth
and eventually reach a height of 450ft, giving
panoramic views, out to sea and inland. The
paths go on to Lee, a pretty hamlet nestling in
Borough Valley, a deep combe full of fuchsias.

On the eastern edge of Ilfracombe, just off
the A399 Combe Martin road, is
Chambercombe Manor, an ancient manor
house, with some Elizabethan additions,
containing a collection of period furniture and
set in lovely gardens with wildfowl ponds.
Half a mile further along the A399 stands the
Old Corn Mill, a 16th-century watermill with
an 18ft overshot waterwheel restored to
working order; wholemeal flour is ground and
sold and the mill contains an interesting
selection of old machinery.

The road to **Combe Martin** climbs out of
Ilfracombe and then drops towards the village
at the harbour. The village stretches for 2 miles
inland along the River Umber, with a few short
lanes off the long main street – variously
known as Borough Road, King Street, High
Street, Castle Street and finally Victoria Street.
Whatever the name there is little of
architectural interest on the road apart from a
hotel, 'The Pack of Cards', built in the 18th
century by a local gambler, George Ley, after a
prolonged winning streak. Each of its four
storeys has 13 doors, and the whole building

Ilfracombe

Combe Martin Wildlife Park

Higher Leigh Manor, just outside Combe Martin, has experienced an oddly chequered history. In the cellars of the present house are the only remains of a medieval monastic building, a remote chapel. After the dissolution the manor house was built over the old foundations. In 1940 the building reverted to religious use when an order of nuns moved in; during the last War they welcomed a gang of evacuees from London. The most recent owners have created a monkey sanctuary.

From a modest start in 1970 the enterprise has developed to incorporate a diverse selection of wildlife, tropical plants and rare trees. In addition to recreating as natural a habitat as possible for the six breeding species of monkeys, there are wallabies, seals and otters; there is also a children's zoo with more familiar livestock to be visited.

A surprising attraction is the huge 'OO' gauge model railway display, complete with towns, villages and mountain scenery. The real outlook is superb, too, with views from the grounds overlooking the village of Combe Martin and the North Devon coast.

originally had 52 windows, representing the suits and number of cards in a pack.

The Combe Martin Motorcycle Collection, in the village, will delight enthusiasts of early motoring; a collection of old and new British bikes is displayed, together with posters, pumps and advertising from garages of the 1930s and 40s.

The main attraction of the village is the harbour itself, surrounded by steep-sided wooded cliffs; at low tide the Umber rushes out from a culvert under the street into a pebbly channel down the beach. Beneath the cliffs, rock-pools attract children with buckets and fishing nets.

The main road zig-zags upwards out of the village and inland towards Exmoor; it meets the A39 at Blackmoor Gate, where a left turn leads to Lynton and Lynmouth. There is an alternative, coastal route which involves driving around some of the narrowest and steepest lanes in Devon, a route well worth taking if you want to walk along some of the most stunning and beautiful coast, woods and combes on the north coast – **Trentishoe** and **Holdstone Down**; **Heddon's Mouth**; **Woody Bay** and the **Valley of the Rocks**. The National Trust owns most of this coastline; car-parks and footpaths are well marked at all of the sites.

To follow the coastal route from Combe Martin, go up the High Street and turn left along Shute Lane. At Stoney Corner turn left again towards Trentishoe, this road passing over the saddle between Holdstone and Trentishoe Down. **Holdstone Down** rises to 1143ft at its highest point, giving views across the Bristol Channel to Wales, and inland to Exmoor. The road through Trentishoe leads steeply down to the River Heddon at Hunter's Inn, set in mature woodland; a path continues on to Heddon's Mouth – here the woodland thins to reveal heather-covered slopes converging at a stony beach, the river rushing over smooth pebbles into the sea. A beautifully restored lime kiln stands almost in the sea where limestone was landed from Wales, turned into lime, and used to counteract the acidity of the local soil. Paths run on both sides of the river, starting to the right of the inn, or back along the Trentishoe road, giving an easy and varied walk. The most energetic track climbs Heddon's Mouth Cleave by leaving the path on the west of the river about halfway to the mouth.

The lane to the right of Hunter's Inn leads to Lynton via Martinhoe and Woody Bay which are accessible only on foot; there is a sandy beach at low tide, another old lime kiln and the remains of a jetty, built to attract the paddle steamers that once took holidaymakers on trips along the channel.

About a mile west of Lynton the lane passes through the Valley of the Rocks: steeply curved heathland surmounted by precarious rock formations, standing like ancient fortresses overlooking the sea and moors. (Approaching this route from Lynton, take the road past the town hall at the top of the village westwards to the valley.)

As a small scattered farming settlement, **Lynton** has been in existence since prehistoric times. The surrounding common land encouraged sheep farming, and by the late 18th century spinning was the principal occupation. Both Lynton and Lynmouth were 'discovered' as holiday resorts at the time of the Napoleonic wars, when people were turning to England for their recreation, much of Europe being closed to travellers.

Crowning the brow of the hill, Lynton is perched some 600ft above its smaller twin village of **Lynmouth**, which nestles at the foot of the great rounded cliffs below. The name is derived from the Anglo-Saxon 'hlynna' a torrent; Lynton – the town on the Lyn, and Lynmouth, the mouth of the torrent. The magnificent setting has been much praised: Southey referred to it as the 'English Switzerland', and Gainsborough described the area as 'the most delightful place for a landscape painter this country can boast'. Most of the notable architecture of Lynton is Victorian and Edwardian, epitomised by the splendid town hall, on Lee Road, which also houses the tourist information office, and serves as an excellent point from which to begin an exploration of the town. Built early this century, it was financed by the publisher, George Newnes, to celebrate his son's coming of age. Newnes's bust in the entrance hall was unveiled by Sir Arthur Conan Doyle. Newnes was a great local benefactor and was responsible for many schemes to improve both Lynton and Lynmouth; he backed the construction of the narrow-gauge railway from Barnstaple to Lynton, which operated from 1898 to 1935, and sponsored the cliff railway, which links the two villages. He lived in Hollerday House, on the hill behind the town hall. The house has now been demolished, but the grounds are a public park, with a path leading to the Valley of the Rocks, and superb views along the coast.

Lynmouth cliff railway

From the Town Hall, walk down Lee Road to Queen Street. This steep road, little more than an alley, used to be the main street of Lynton before the 18th century and the redevelopment of the town. It is flanked by souvenir shops, a few catering for the essentials of the locals. The Globe Hotel at the bottom is one of the oldest pubs in Lynton, famed for the wrestling matches that were held in the back yard.

Along to the left opposite the Globe is the old market hall, and on the left-hand side of the road on the corner is whitewashed St Vincent's Cottage, reputed to be one of the oldest cottages in Lynton, dating from the early 18th century, now housing the Lyn and

Exmoor Museum. The exhibits reflect the occupations and trade of the local community, a veritable conglomeration of ephemera, all found a place – stuffed birds, a dolls' house, ancient tools and Doone china. The house itself is delightful, and was saved from demolition in 1962 to be run as the museum.

Bear left from the museum up the hill past the old Smithy; at the top, the route to the right continues around Castle Hill, past the Castle Hotel, with views up the coast and across to Wales on a clear day; it returns to the town via Northwalk Hill and thence to St Mary's church. The church is not particularly inspiring; it dates partly from the 13th century, but most was rebuilt in Victorian times, and bears the drab formality imposed by well-wishing 'restorers'. From the churchyard, however, there are spectacular views; an orientation table helps identify features on the Welsh coast.

Off Lee Road, the famous cliff railway offers a hair-raising and precipitous descent to **Lynmouth**. The railway is water-powered. Two carriages are counter-balanced by huge 700-gallon water tanks. When the tank of the top carriage is filled, and the brakes released, gravity comes into action, and the bottom carriage – its tank empty – is hauled up the 1 in 1.75 slope. There is a zig-zag path down the verdant cliffside for the weak-hearted.

Mars Hill, the oldest part of Lynmouth, with its creeper-covered cottages, frames the cliffs behind the Esplanade; this was where R D Blackmore stayed whilst researching *Lorna Doone*.

Further along is the Lynmouth Flood Memorial hall: a tragic reminder of the fateful night in 1952, when, after a particularly wet summer, a sudden violent storm was all that was needed to cause the sponge-like mass of Exmoor to release its load and send a flash flood of unprecedented scale raging down the

The Hanging Stone
A great slab of granite forms one of the boundary marks of Combe Martin parish; known as the Hanging Stone, its name is derived from a local legend.

A thief stole a sheep and tied the poor animal up with a rope that he then tied round his own neck. Resting from his exertions he leant on the stone; the sheep struggled, clambered over the stone and fell off. The man was yanked off his feet and strangled. North Dartmoor, Sidmouth and other parts of the country all have stones with similar names, and similar stories to explain their origins.

The stone is more likely to be a Saxon marker, a standing stone.

Quince Honey Farm
A unique attraction on the western edge of South Molton, this is the largest wild-bee farm in the world; visitors can watch bees in their natural state from the safety of glass booths and tunnels.

The building housing the bees has been especially designed to facilitate the work of the beekeepers and to maximise the viewing area for the public, whilst leaving the bees as free as possible to continue their activities; it has proved so successful and allowed such detailed observation that new discoveries in the theory and practice of beekeeping have been made.

Observation hives enable visitors to see young bees and larvae still incarcerated in the sealed cells of the comb, whilst the drones and workers hurry about their business. The queen, at the centre of attention and difficult to spot in the melee of buzzing bodies, lays eggs to build up and maintain her hive of some 60,000 bees. The shop naturally specialises in all varieties of honey, including the local favourite, heather-flavoured; pure beeswax is also available, either made up into candles on the premises or in tins as a fine wood polish.

East and West Lyn rivers, devastating the village of Lynmouth in the middle of the night. The river hurtled down the main street carrying huge boulders and tree trunks: ninety houses were destroyed and thirty-four people lost their lives. Since then there have been extensive schemes to prevent such a tragedy occurring again, and the confines of the river have been heavily reinforced. The Hall has an exhibition of photographs recording the tragedy, and scenes of the village before and after.

Another stormy night is featured in the folklore of Lynmouth: in the winter of 1899 a full-rigged ship, the *Forest Hall*, was in difficulties off Porlock. The seas were too severe for the lifeboat to be launched from Lynmouth, so the decision was taken to haul the boat to the more sheltered harbour at Porlock; the 13-mile journey involved 10½ hours of back-breaking labour as the 3½ ton boat was dragged by teams of horses up the 1:4 slope of Countisbury Hill; gangs of men went ahead to hack down trees and widen the road as they went. The effort was rewarded: the entire crew of the stricken boat were rescued.

Tucked behind the Riverside Road, Lynmouth Street is now sadly packed with souvenir shops, with little to commend them. Cross the river by the footbridge to a large grassy sward and public gardens, complete with deck chairs, putting green, and ample shady trees. From here there is a delightful vista of the village. Perched precariously on the cliffside like nesting gulls, hang gabled Victorian hotels, peeping from verdant hideouts. Any further development has fortunately been restricted by the nature of the topography, and Lynmouth retains an air of the Victorian era.

The foot of Countisbury Hill shelters the shingle beach, with rock pools and shells to be discovered. Back towards the harbour on the right of the river mouth is a salmon 'engine'. This device is made from wattle hurdles used to trap the fish, and is reputed to be one of two still operating in England. On the breakwater is the Rhenish Tower – an unusual construction, so called because it was modelled on similar structures found on the Rhine. It is in fact a replica of the original, built in the early 19th century, but destroyed in the flood. It contained a water tank to take sea water to the home of a local colonel for his bath.

SOUTH MOLTON

Standing amongst wooded hillsides on the River Mole, the town of **South Molton** still thrives as a market for the livestock of the area, acting as a gateway from the rugged hills of Exmoor in the north. The town dates from the early Saxon period and rose to importance during medieval times; in the 16th century it was made a borough and a bishopric, thriving not only as a market but also as a staging post and a centre for woollen weaving and the mining industry. During the 19th century its importance declined as the North Devon railway bypassed the town depriving it of much lucrative trade.

The main car-park occupies the large open market place, behind the pannier market, through which is the town centre. The pannier market was built in 1863, a voluminous hall, the roof and clerestory raised on slender cast-iron columns forming aisles on each side for traders' stalls; the produce market here still attracts 60 to 70 stallholders. Leave through the impressive arched entrance surmounted by three giant carved ram's heads – the view opens out into the appropriately named Broad Street, an elongated town square running east-west, with many attractive Georgian façades, although these often hide much older structures.

Next door to the market is the impressive

Exmoor – peregrine falcon

town hall, built on three arches over the pavement. Although dating from 1743, many of its architectural features are in an older style having been purchased from Stowe mansion, a house belonging to the Earls of Bath at Kilkhampton in Cornwall. The town hall contains the South Molton Museum, exhibiting many artefacts from the local trades: mining, wool, and agriculture, with a continuous slide show relating the history of the town.

Continuing along Broad Street: on the right is the George Hotel, decorated with actors' masks, dating from the inn's time as a theatre tavern where travelling companies performed. Although the façade is quite narrow, the property stretches on and on back from the road, filling the ancient burgage plot, a relict feature of the medieval town plan.

Crossing Broad Street: opposite the town hall is New Walk Steps, leading to the Parish Church of St Mary Magdalene, crowning a hill that was once the centre of the town. Little remains of a 13th-century church which was built on the site but fell into disrepair due to the demands of the Bishop of Exeter for funds to build the new Cathedral. The present church resembles a small Cathedral, its 15th-century tower rising to 140ft; it includes interesting medieval carvings and 15th-century pulpit. It nearly became a Cathedral when in 1535 the town was created a bishopric, but the cost of maintaining a more prestigious religious position was too much for the town and a bishop was never appointed.

South Molton is still a busy and active town, one of the main reasons being that a new trade has come to replace the old: there are a dozen antique businesses selling worldwide as well as catering to passing tourists and offering everything from fine art to bric-à-brac, making a walk round the town well worth while.

Leaving South Molton eastwards along the

A361, turn left into Station Road and follow the road to **North Molton**. A sleepy agricultural town, its history centres on mining: iron and copper mainly, but gold, silver and lead were also found. In 1874 a mineral line was cut along the valley to carry the ore to the now disused South Molton station and this is a pleasant walk between the two towns.

All Saints, the parish church, has a fine sandstone tower of 100ft, and inside the 15th-century font and pulpit are notable, with, for Devon, the unusual feature of a clerestoried nave.

From South Molton, **Bampton** is about 16 miles to the east, on the A361. Situated at the junction of the verdant mid-Devon valleys and the rising ground of Exmoor, Bampton lies on the River Batherm, and two ancient trackways meet: north-south and east-west, now the A396 and A361. The Saxon village developed into a small town in the 13th century, reaching the height of its prosperity in the early 19th century with a thriving cloth industry; its two fairs were then amongst the biggest in the west. The Georgian-style houses which now predominate date from this time. Now a quiet, pleasing backwater, it comes to life in late October when the Exmoor Pony Sale takes place: Landrovers, shooting-sticks and headscarves appear at every corner; country characters survey the horseflesh, while the ponies stamp and flick their long tails.

The future of the Exmoor Pony Sale is far from certain. Some oppose the occasion and find it unpleasant. Others maintain that it is a thoroughly traditional event that should be cherished.

Tucked behind the main road, the church of St Michael and All Angels occupies what was probably a pagan religious site. St Michael, the archangel who cast down Satan, is frequently commemorated in this way. It is mainly 14th-century with 15th-century additions.

Church font, North Molton

Next to the main south door is a fine medieval window, moved, restored and redecorated to commemorate the Bampton dead in the First World War. On the west wall of the tower is a curious memorial to the Clerk's son who died in 1776 when an icicle fell on him from the tower –

Bless this little
iiiii
Here he lies
In a sad pickle
Kill'd by icicle.

Following the Exe valley south on the A396, turn onto the A373 at Tiverton west to **Witheridge**, lying on the high mid-Devon plateau; much of the parish is over 600ft above sea-level. The countryside is characterised by gently rolling farmland bisected by the valleys of the Little Dart river and several small streams.

Witheridge Moors were first inhabited some 3000 years ago, and two Bronze Age burial mounds survive. By the time of the Domesday survey, the parish boasted 12 manors, as well as numerous other smaller dwellings, establishing a community of some importance. By 1550 it held borough status, and local fairs and markets provided a framework for the close-knit agricultural community. In the late 19th century, local directories indicate that Witheridge was a self-sufficient little town, with a good range of shops and facilities, and seven public houses within the parish. As communications improved, however, Witheridge fell into decline, and now it acts more as a dormitory town to the larger centres of Tiverton and South Molton. But there is still a pervasive village atmosphere in the centre, where the large Square retains the charm of bygone splendour and prosperity, and the cottages around seem to have evolved in a somewhat haphazard fashion, far removed from the careful structured planning of the unattractive new estates on the edge of the village.

Leave Witheridge on the A373 back towards Tiverton and take the B3042 right to **Eggesford** on the River Taw. Eggesford is part of an estate that belonged to the Copplestone family in the 16th century. All that is left is the church, All Saints, which contains two of the finest monuments in Devon: one to Viscount Chichester and the Copplestone heiress whom he married, so acquiring the estate; and one to Arthur Chichester, Earl of Donegal, and his two wives. All round Eggesford are Forestry Commission plantations with many walks down to the River Taw, through older deciduous woods as well as the more modern conifers.

Continue north along the A377 towards Barnstaple; take the right hand turning to **Chulmleigh**. Once a bustling market town on the main route from Barnstaple to Exeter, it declined in the 19th century, with the development of the turnpike road along the Taw Valley (now the A377) and the arrival of the railway in 1854, when the markets were transferred to more convenient locations. It occupies a prominent hilltop site overlooking the Little Dart river to the south, with far-stretching views to Dartmoor. It became a borough in the mid-13th century, and reached the height of its prosperity in the 17th and 18th centuries, with a thriving woollen industry, market and cattle fairs.

Now, the town centre remains delightfully unspoilt, with a handful of shops catering for all the day-to-day needs of the locals, as well as the ubiquitous pubs and small café. A friendly atmosphere pervades, and fresh crusty clotted cream is scooped from a big enamel bowl in the delicatessen.

Although much of the town was severely damaged by a fire in 1803, there are still many

Cider

Cider, or 'scrumpy' as it is known in Devon, was traditionally made on almost every farm, not to be sold but for the family, and as payment to workers.

Traditional cider-making was an art, with jealously guarded secrets handed down from father to son; many farmers still use the ancient mills and presses of their forebears and follow the old ways to produce a drink as high in alcohol and as clear as good wine.

In autumn the apples from the cider orchards are raked into heaps and left to 'sweat' in the grass as fermentation begins; those that turn black and rotten are discarded, but the rest are carted back to the farm to be milled or ground into a thick 'pomace'. Layer upon layer of crushed apple, contained within beds of straw or horse-hair cloths, is piled on to a great press; as pressure is exerted the rich brown fluid begins to flow. The juice is immediately transferred into large vats where it remains until a frothing 'head' has risen, usually after two or three days; it is then drawn off into casks, and left to ferment. When fermentation ceases, the cider is ready to drink. Vintage cider may be kept for a year or two and some say it improves with ageing.

Until recently, during the hay and corn harvests each labourer was allowed on an average a gallon of cider a day. Many farms still produce cider, and it can be bought direct, but beware of its strength.

attractive old cottages; the Barnstaple Inn dates from 1633. Off the main street run little alleys, glimpses of colour-washed cottages and tumbling nasturtiums, children's toys and barking dogs.

A charming cobbled lane opening into a square with a cluster of houses leads from the High Street to the church, magnificently situated on the south-western edge of the town. Although there is no record of the first church to be built here, a fragment of an ancient Celtic cross now over the south porch suggests that there was definitely some place of worship here by the 11th century. The present building dates from the 15th century, and was once an important collegiate church, founded by Isabella de Fortibus, Countess of Devon, to provide stipends for seven canons. Local legend expounds that she rescued seven babies born at one time to a local couple, who in desperation planned to drown them all in the Little Dart. Isabella brought them up, and when they reached manhood they became prebends of the church.

The interior is dominated by the superb rood screen – 50ft of carved oak stretching right across the church, dividing the Sanctuary and Choir stalls from the nave, and surmounted by coloured wooden figures representing the four evangelists. Fine wagon roofs span the nave and aisles, with carved bosses and delightfully crude figures of angels with wings outstretched. The tower, with its massive buttresses, rises 86ft, in four gradually diminishing stages; at the base are the huge granite blocks of the west doorway, with its finely carved and moulded headstone.

Returning to the main A377 continue north and turn left at Kingford and then right onto the B3217 to **High Bickington**. The prefix 'High' is very appropriate as the views north-east to Exmoor and south to Dartmoor are ousatnding.

A Saxon settlement, the village belonged to a Saxon nobleman, Britric, at the time of the Conquest. Unfortunately for him, whilst on a diplomatic mission to Flanders he refused the hand of the Duke's daughter Matilda, who later married William the Conqueror, so she reaped her revenge by taking his lands and imprisoning him at Winchester. Subsequent history is less eventful and it is now an attractive agricultural centre.

The church of St Mary makes a visit here of real value. The church itself is largely unrestored, beyond some changes in the 16th century and can be dated back to the 12th century.

The treasures of the church are the 70 or so pew ends from two periods: Late Gothic with simple tracery (13th century) and Renaissance with saints, apostles and lay figures (16th century); the detail and skill of the carvings is exceptional. Some have cryptic designs on them, for example, an inverted 'V' – a mason's mark, and an alpha and omega motif; at one time professions and families rented pews and these may be signs of that wardship. Note also the wonderful tapestry work of the modern kneelers.

Return to the A377 and continue towards Barnstaple. At Umberleigh turn right and after about 2 miles left to **Chittlehampton** – 'dwellers in the hollow' (or cietel) – so, unlike High Bickington, it is hidden in sheltering hills and rolling pasture. 'Chittlehampton for beauty' runs the local saying, and this is a beautiful place. Dominating the village is the 15th-century church uniquely dedicated to St Hieritha, originally Urith, a Celtic maiden who was born a mile north of the village, at Stowford, and probably lived in the early 8th century. She was accused of causing a drought in the area and savagely hacked to death by the local farmers with their scythes. St Hieritha is remembered by a holy well, and by the

Chittlehampton – Pyrenean lily, perhaps introduced by monks

miracle of the well's appearance as she died:

Where the holy maiden fell
Water gushed forth from a well,
And the dry earth blossomed.

The well still exists at the eastern end of the village, although the original building surrounding it has been demolished. She was buried nearby and some time later the first church was built over her remains. A tunnel of pollarded lime trees leads up to the south porch of the present church, which has the finest tower in Devon: 114ft high and crowned with delicate tracery, combining the solidity of Devon towers with the grace of Somerset's.

Hartland Point

5 North-West Devon

North-west Devon is a marshy upland,
bordered on the north and west by the sea, to
the south by Dartmoor and to the east the
valley of the River Torridge. Due to its wet and
rugged topography it has not experienced the
modernisation of farming that the more fertile
areas to the south have enjoyed and, because
of its relative lack of sandy beaches and poor
accessibility, has not developed as a major
tourist area; thus it remains characteristically
old-fashioned. The only major centre of
population is Bideford, once a major port: its
shallow quayside is only able now to take the
smallest of today's merchant vessels. The rest
of the region consists of scattered villages and
hamlets, surrounded by damp heathland and
fields. Narrow lanes criss-cross the area to
reveal small farm cottages, and a handful of
holiday homes.

The main roads keep to the high ground,
often following the routes of ancient
ridgeways; turning off there is often a sudden
descent into a narrow valley, or in the north
down a precipitous cliff road to the sea. A
number of rivers rise from the upland plateau:
the Tamar threads its way south skirting the
Dartmoor mass and reaching the sea at
Plymouth, most of its journey forming the
boundary between Devon and Cornwall. The
other major river is the Torridge, which
although rising only ten miles, as the crow
flies, from its mouth, follows a devious route of
some fifty-three miles; it flows south but
baulks at the rising ground of Dartmoor, then
performs a U-turn to head north-east, to the
sea at Bideford Bay. It may have originally
continued south, but due to upheavals in the
earth's crust Dartmoor rose, a huge dome-
shaped mass, and diverted its course.

At the coast the uplands dramatically fall
away, creating some of the most spectacular

Bideford

Population: 13,993

Early Closing: Wed

Market Day: Sat

Cashpoints: *Barclays* 84 High St; *Lloyds* 5 High St; *Midland* 16 High St; *NatWest* 86 High St

Tourist Information: The Quay (summer only)

Attraction: Burton Art Gallery

By Road: London 225 miles (A39, A361, M5, M4), Barnstaple 9 miles (A39)

By Rail: The nearest station is at Barnstaple, 1hr 10mins from Exeter

scenery in Devon. The Somerset and North Devon Coast Path, which can be joined at numerous places, gives the visitor the chance to explore windswept clifftops and hidden valleys. Between Hartland Point and the boundary with Cornwall the coast runs north-south, facing the full force of the Atlantic and prevailing westerly winds. The resulting erosion has left a line of jagged cliffs with razor-edged fingers of rock reaching into the sea. The distinctive strata have become twisted into strange angles. From Hartland Point to Westward Ho! the coastline is more protected and the cliffs less sheer, often covered in trees and scrub which soften their outline; steep-sided wooded combes are cut by quick-flowing streams that tumble down the cliffs to the sea. The erosion of the land has meant that in some places these streams have lost their valleys and cascade down the cliffs from a considerable height. One can be seen from Clovelly and there are others at Welcome and Speke's Mill. Traditional sea-based economic activities survive: boat-building in Appledore, merchant ships trading from Bideford and fishing for mackerel from Clovelly and Buck's Mill.

BIDEFORD
Bideford stands near the mouth of the River Torridge, beyond sand and salt marshes which prevent an easy crossing. This has meant that from the Iron Age, Bideford (by-the-ford) developed as an important staging post on the North Devon highway. The first bridge across the river was built around 1300; made from wood, it had two chapels on it, no doubt because it was built from contributions promoted by the Bishops of Exeter. The bridge 'feoffees' held an annual dinner on the bridge, a great event in the local calendar, a tradition which sadly ended in the last century.

A stone bridge was erected over and around the wooden one during the 15th century, and much remains, although it has been widened and strengthened frequently since then. This might explain why it is claimed that none of its 24 arches have the same span.

The quay, which runs north from the bridge, was built in the 17th century and Bideford became an important port for over 100 years. Trade with the Americas flourished; tobacco from Virginia and Maryland was landed here, and because of inland trade routes, Bideford thrived.

The quay is the place to start a tour of the town; near the bridge the large library and Bridge Hall form an impressive entrance to Bideford; along the quay the façades of the buildings conjure up the cramped busy bustle of the port in its heyday. Merchant vessels moor at the quay and jostle with pleasure craft. At the northern end is a statue of Charles Kingsley, the author of *Westward Ho!*, part of which he wrote at North Down House, in the Strand.

The quay ends at the entrance to Victoria Park which continues along the waterfront. In the park are the Armada Guns reputed to have been captured from the Spanish in 1588. The connection with the Armada centres around Sir Richard Grenville who fought alongside Raleigh. The Grenville family were lords of the manor of Bideford for over 700 years; William the Conqueror granted Richard de Granville the lordship, and many of the family had distinguished military careers. The Burton Art Gallery on the edge of the park displays a good collection of work by the watercolour artist Hubert Coop, including many local scenes; there is also a collection of Bideford pottery – mainly 19th-century yellow slipware with sgraffito decoration. The town rises up from the quay in a series of narrow streets which although having a certain amount of architectural interest have suffered from

Lundy – puffin

unsympathetic modernisation. However, some of the buildings reveal the past prosperity of the town with impressive bow fronts and decorated reliefs.

Further down the river, where it joins the Taw, lies **Appledore**, in the estuary. Leave Bideford at Victoria Park, along Kingsley Road; take the A386 via Northam. It was described by Charles Kingsley as the 'little white fishing village', built on a steep hillside facing east across the estuary of the Torridge to Instow; here the Torridge and Taw meet and, through a channel narrowed by Braunton Burrows on the north, and Northam Burrows on the south, they flow into the broad bay.

Climbing up from the quayside, Appledore is criss-crossed with picturesque, narrow lanes, closely packed with cottages. The cottages are brightly painted, with hanging baskets and tubs of flowers, creating a patchwork of colours. West Appledore, towards the mouth of the estuary, consists of one street, Irsha Street, where small two-up and two-down cottages back directly onto the river; on the shore side are a series of 'courts', with even tinier cottages facing each other across cobbled yards; these were the homes of fishermen and shipwrights.

Traditional boat-building and fishing industries survive: the boatyards are at the southern end of the quay, at one time numerous, providing employment for many. The wealthy shipbuilders lived in the grand houses on Marine Parade. The Quay continues to be a workplace: there are crab pots and nets laid out awaiting the fishing boats; the salmon fishery in the estuary has been productive since Saxon times, and visiting boats moor at the Quay beside Appledore's shops and shoreside hostelries. Towards the top of the town, in Odun Street, is the North Devon Maritime Museum, with fabulous views over the estuary. Once the home of shipowners and merchants, it is an appropriate place to see the history of seafaring in its many forms, each room portraying a different aspect of maritime life.

With the estuary on the right, leave Appledore on the Torridge Road, and follow the coast for 2 miles to the south-west; here, situated at the neck of a great spit of sand jutting into the estuary, lies **Westward Ho!**

Until 1855, following the publication of Charles Kingsley's famous novel, which supplied the name, the region was regarded as a dull area of sand and marshy wasteland, but a consortium of local businessmen, recognising its potential, chose it to be developed as a holiday site, and formed a company to create the 'new resort'. The Countess of Portsmouth laid the foundation stone of what is now the Golden Bay Hotel (formerly the Royal); a church was built, and two or three rows of cottages, with several large scattered Victorian villas. Unfortunately, things did not work to plan: the pier and some of the houses were washed away in a storm, and the place was left prey to piecemeal speculators, hence the hotch-potch of development and architectural style. The remaining Victorian architecture is good, although generally in a bad state of decay, having, for the most part, been converted to holiday flats – notably the Kingsley College for Sons of Noblemen and Gentlemen, originally built as a school. Even the chapel has succumbed to the pressures and been converted to holiday accommodation.

Charles Kingsley

Despite its faults, Westward Ho! has plenty to offer the holidaymaker. Beyond the statutory handful of shops catering for the seasonal trade in ice-cream, rock, chips and buckets and spades, the site itself is spectacular: the great rounded bracken- and tree-covered hillside rises behind the resort, with terraced rows, detached villas and brightly painted beach huts looking out over two miles or so of sand stretching to the mouth of the Torridge and Taw estuary. The sands are backed by a pebble ridge, 50ft wide and some 20ft high, of smooth grey oval stones, some the size of dinner plates. Winter storms throw some of the pebbles over the bank to the grassy Burrows, where they are collected and replaced by 'Potwallopers' – immortalised by Rudyard Kipling in *Stalky and Co.*, an account of his schooldays here at the United Services College. In 1927, the cliff walks he explored as a boy were named in his honour, the Kipling Tors, now owned by the National Trust. Situated at the western end of the village, the track along the bottom of the Tors is part of a disused railway; it closed in 1917, having operated for only 16 years. The most spectacular views are from the old Coastguard Lookout, used to watch for ships in peril, or invading fleets. From here it is possible to see all of Bideford Bay, with the island of Lundy on the horizon, and the promontories of Hartland to the west; Baggy Point is to the north, with the Taw/Torridge estuary between, and the hills of Exmoor stretch away in the distance.

Beneath the final section of the walk looking over the cliff edge is a 'raised beach' – a platform of rock some 25 feet above the present shore-line, on which lies a band of pebbles, now stranded on what was the ancient beach, caused by a drop in sea level at the time of the Ice Age.

Perhaps the best reason for visiting Westward Ho! is to explore **Northam Burrows**, 650 acres of low-lying saltmarsh area nestling against sand dunes behind the great pebble ridge, and rough sparse pasture, grazed by a few hardy sheep and ponies. The site, now run as a Country Park by the County Council, boasts the oldest golf links course in England, established in 1864. Its isolation and relative inaccessibility have prevented its promotion to a championship course. A comprehensive visitors' centre has recently opened towards the farthest end of the car-park, with an excellent display of the flora, fauna and geology of the area, with reconstructed rock pools and a pictorial history of the Burrows. The ample car-park relieves the centre of Westward Ho! and also enables visitors to enjoy the farther end of the beach without the additional effort of lugging all the necessary paraphernalia along the ridge or across the sand. Although at low tide the expanse of sand is vast, because of the very gentle gradient it all but disappears at high water, forcing the beach visitors to be herded up towards the pebble ridge, totally altering the feeling of space experienced only hours before.

Note that bathing at the far end of the Burrows near the mouth of the estuary is dangerous, with very strong currents around the sand bar.

BUCK'S MILLS

The A39 from Bideford follows the north coast, climbing up from the Torridge along the edge of the upland region. Leave Bideford southwards with the river on the left, and turn sharp right a little after the bridge. About 10 miles along this road is Buck's Cross; turn right here to visit **Buck's Mills**, a small fishing village clinging to the coast. A winding tree-lined lane leads down to a car-park at the top of the village, and it is a short walk to the pretty cottages; a steep track leads down to the stone quay where local fishermen work on their boats and store their nets and tackle. There are magnificent views along the coast to Abbotsham in the east, and to the west round the whole sweep of steeply wooded cliffs past Clovelly to the sharp headland of Gallantry Bower. Noticeable below the village is a vast buttress, looking like an ancient castle, but in fact a disused lime kiln.

From Buck's Mills there are several walks to

Cob

It may be hard to believe but many thousands of the buildings in Devon are little more than mud huts! Cob, the most widely used building material until the middle of the last century, consists of clay earth and water, with small stones, straw hair and cow dung added as binders. The ingredients were trodden into a malleable consistency either by horses or by men on the house site.

A stone plinth of anything from two to six feet wide was made and the cob shovelled on in two-feet layers, trodden down and left for a week to dry. Then another layer was added, and this was repeated until the wall was finished. The rough surface was hacked smooth when dry, and generally plastered. Whitewash or colour-wash was applied later. Many unpainted cob structures can be seen, usually farm buildings or garden walls, revealing the local geology: a dull, rich red in the sandstone areas and a mellow buff in the clay region. The malleability of cob has created the rounded and bulging shapes that give Devon buildings their character.

Cob is a very durable material if the top and bottom are kept dry, as damp tends to turn it back to earth, but the greatest danger to cob is modern building technology. Rendering with cement stops the cob from breathing so it retains moisture and can crumble, whereas the old lime render let the moisture both in and out thus keeping it stable.

be recommended: the coastal path eastwards has spectacular vistas from the coastguard's lookout; another walk from the car-park, marked 'Short Woodland Walk', follows the stream up the valley until it reaches a pretty waterfall.

Three-and-a-half miles past the turning to Buck's Mills on the A39, is the B3237 to **Clovelly**. Bear right at the Clovelly Cross roundabout, and follow the road for 2 miles. Vehicle access to Clovelly is restricted, so park in the car-park.

Take the steepest hillside with which you are acquainted; let the Atlantic roll at its base; cover it with ancient trees and tangled undergrowth to its summit . . . people its banks with a straggling village of irregularly shaped lichen-covered cottages, on so sharp an incline that the base of the one is on a level with the roof of its neighbour; pave the street with miniature boulders . . . and terminate the descent by an antique pier of wave-worn stones . . . and then you will obtain something which would resemble Clovelly, if it were not indeed unique . . . and did not surpass all descriptive powers.

Charles Kingsley's description of Clovelly in the last century applies equally today; despite commercialisation, the old village has avoided modernisation and remains a delight. Its precipitous position makes car access impossible and the Hamlyn family, who owned the village for many generations, followed by the Clovelly Estate Company, have ensured that no major alterations have been allowed to spoil this idyllic spot.

The biggest change is that Clovelly has become the chief tourist attraction of the region, and so is usually packed with day-trippers; however, it is such a uniquely beautiful place that this should not deter anyone from discovering its narrow lanes and magical atmosphere.

At the car-park at the top of the village are a

new visitors' centre, self-service restaurant,
audio-visual theatre, gift shop and toilets. It is
an inauspicious introduction, resembling a
motorway service station, and just as
expensive. But leaving the centre on foot – no
cars are able to negotiate the village – you
enter a remarkable world. The dense collection
of white cottages, piled almost one on top of
the other on either side of the stepped and
cobbled lane, lead down to the harbourside. In
the summer, the place is a blaze of colour as
villagers vie for the best display in their
window boxes and tubs. Giant fuchsias, almost
wild, and honeysuckle cover the walls of some
of the tiny cottages.

The 14th century quay curls round to
enclose a crescent of calm water; the view
along the coast and back up the village are
enchanting. Many visitors elect to take the path
straight down to the bottom, leaving
exploration of the hidden courts and lanes to
their return journey when pauses to stop and
admire become an essential opportunity to
regain strength and breath for the rest of the
climb. It is very steep. Alternatively, a
Landrover regularly takes tired visitors up via a
track through Clovelly Court.

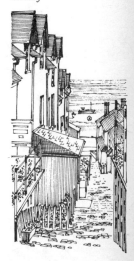

Clovelly

Another way to reach Clovelly, and one
that is well worth the small charge, is via
Hobby Drive. The entrance is at a lodge set in
a wooded area about 1½ miles beyond Buck's
Cross travelling from Bideford. It is a 3-mile
long stony track that winds through thick
woodland clinging to the side of the cliffs. Now
and then there are glimpses of the coastline,
and it is worth stopping to take in the view,
especially at a point where there are a few
white-painted seats as the view of Clovelly,
hundreds of feet below, whets the appetite for
a closer look. The drive was cut in the last
century, given its name because it was the
hobby of the then owner of Clovelly, Sir James
Hamlyn Williams.

Clotted Cream

Thick and crusty, rich and yellow, Devonshire clotted cream is like no other; taste it with a traditional cream tea of warm scones and strawberry jam – home-made of course; in Devon the cream is spread thickly on halves of scones like butter.

Many farmers' wives still make their own clotted cream and it is well worth searching out the real thing; alternatively try making your own: it is not a complicated process.

Full cream milk is strained into a shallow pan containing about half a pint of water to prevent the milk from adhering to the sides; it is allowed to stand for twelve or twenty-four hours. Then it is scalded by very gradual heating to 180°F, usually achieved by moving it inch by inch towards a fire; after about 50 minutes the cream separates, forming a bubbly froth over the surface. In a traditional farmhouse the pan was then removed to the larder or dairy, a cool place where the cream could solidify; a skimmer was then used to lift the crust off the thin milk left below in the pan.

Country dairies and even some village butchers sell cream fresh from the pan and many provide a speedy postal service, dispatching little metal tubs of cream all over the country.

The Hamlyn family made a habit of creating odd pathways and follies and many can be discovered along a path beginning near the top entrance to the cobbled street at Clovelly. With the exit from Hobby Drive and the lane down to Clovelly on your right, to the left is the back lane to the Red Lion. On the left down this lane pass through a large gate and follow the path nearest the cliff edge. Highlights include Angel's Wing, a strangely carved seat with views down the coast; Gallantry Bower, a high windswept headland, and Miss Woodall's seat on a rock balcony overlooking the sea.

Turning right off the main A39 (west-bound) just beyond Clovelly Dykes, it is possible to make an interesting detour incorporating **Hartland Point**, the small town of **Hartland**, **Stoke** and **Hartland Quay** – all well worth a visit.

The road to **Hartland Point** is circuitous and narrow, though well sign-posted, ending in a large field which serves as a car-park; beyond, a track leads to the lighthouse. At this point the coast turns on itself virtually at a right angle, exposing the weird twisted strata of the rocks to the south, with vertical jagged cliffs jutting out to face the full force of the Atlantic. Treacherous to vessels at sea, this point was aptly named by Ptolemy the 'Promontory of Hercules'. To the east the coastline is softer in character, with lower, more rounded contours interspersed by steep wooded combes.

Hartland itself is situated a couple of miles inland, sheltered from the salt spray, if not the wild Atlantic gales. By-passed by the main road, it has not succumbed to the pressures of the tourist trade. It is a rare haven of local activity, bustling as much in mid-winter as at the height of the season. The long main street, flanked by low cottages, leads to a small square, little altered over the centuries. The church of St John, situated in the Square, was built in the 1830s to save Hartland folk the long journey to Stoke, where their parish church is sited. It replaced the old town hall, of which nothing remains save the clock, dating from 1622, and made by John Morecombe of Barnstaple; it is believed to be the oldest pendulum clock in North Devon. Three pubs and a café justify Hartland as a good stopping point for refreshment.

The tiny hamlet of **Stoke**, a couple of miles to the west of Hartland, boasts several fine buildings, including the parish church of St Nectans, (a Welsh missionary who was murdered here in the 6th century). The only remnant of the original building, founded in 1055, is the superb font. The present church, dating from 1360, and little altered, served as a vital landmark to sailors before the lighthouse, with its tower, 128ft high including the pinnacles, tall enough to be seen over the surrounding hills. Internally, both the magnificent rood screen – untouched since it was carved in the 15th century, and the wagon roof – partly panelled and decorated with large, vividly painted stars, should be noted.

Lighthouse, Hartland Point

The Church House, in the Square, was originally occupied by the priests who served at St Nectan's before Hartland Abbey was built in the second half of the 12th century. The Abbey was all but demolished in the dissolution of the monasteries, but fragments of the cloisters were included in the present house down in the valley, which was rebuilt in 1779. It is now open to the public, and houses a unique collection of documents dating from 1160, as well as fine collections of porcelain and furniture. Opening times are restricted, however, so check before visiting.

Hartland Quay is at the end of the road through Stoke – a wild and bleak spot. The building of the quay was authorised by Parliament in 1586, in a bill sponsored by Sir William Courtenay, Sir Walter Raleigh, Sir Francis Drake and Sir John Hawkins. It continued as a busy port for Hartland, shipping coal, lime, granite (from Lundy) and agricultural produce, until the end of the 19th century, when the quay began to break up, and was eventually shattered by the waves, leaving scarcely a trace. The houses at the quay, once inhabited by the dockworkers and limeburners, were converted to a small museum and shop, exhibiting the history of the quay, and portraying the macabre tales of the wrecks along the coast, with numerous exhibits from the stricken ships. The Harbour Master's house, together with offices, stables and storerooms, now form the Hartland Quay Hotel, offering a welcome refuge, especially on a stormy day.

For those in search of a sandy beach (at low tide) and marvellous rock pools, it is worth making the rough descent to the coast at **Welcome**, reached by following the narrow road south from Stoke, offering occasional spectacular views up and down the coast, but for the most part buried deep in wooded valleys. The road peters out, and a rough lane leads down to Welcome Mouth, where there is parking on the grassy sward above the beach. Here, between the heather- and gorse-covered hillside, the stream tumbles in a series of dramatic waterfalls to the beach. This is also an excellent spot to join the coastal footpath, and the scenery to the north is especially beautiful, as is the whole area of interlocking valleys and grassy headlands which make up the widespread village of Welcome, with its few scattered farms, whitewashed cottages and pub. There is a more direct route back to the main road, through the village.

Church font, Hartland

LUNDY

Twelve miles north of Hartland Point lies the island of Lundy, forming a breakwater in the teeth of the westerly winds which whip up the Bristol Channel. It is a lump of granite rock 3½ miles long and ½ mile across, with cliffs rising almost perpendicularly from the shore to 400 or 500ft, like a hunk of moorland dropped in the sea. The name Lundy derives from the Norse word 'Lunde' meaning puffin; the suffix 'ey', means island; so Lundy is Puffin Island.

There is evidence of settlement from the late Stone Age, but its fame grew in the 12th century as the hideout of pirates, ideally placed to attack shipping in the channel. The Marisco family ruled the island until, in June 1242, William de Marisco was hanged, drawn and quartered at Tower Hill, London; his final crime was to finance an attempted assassination of Henry III. The island was then uninhabited, until in the 18th century it again became a haven for privateers and plunderers.

In 1748 the former MP for Barnstaple, Thomas Benson, became the tenant; contracting with the government to transport convicts overseas he landed them on Lundy and set them to work as slave labour. He was discovered only when some of his prisoners escaped to Hartland. Benson was heavily fined and his estates confiscated. To restore his fortunes, he planned a huge insurance swindle: he off-loaded one of his vessels on Lundy and then sank it in order to claim the value of the cargo; unfortunately for him the crew were rescued and the story came out, but Benson managed to escape to Portugal.

Lundy's troubled history improved when William Hudson Heaven bought the island for 9,000 guineas in 1834, building his home there and cultivating the land. From 1834–1918 it became known as the 'Kingdom of Heaven'. Many of the present buildings date from this time, perhaps the most notable example being Millcombe House, now a hotel, which was the Heaven's home; an austere Georgian mansion, it is strangely out of place on this desolate isle. There is the Marisco Tavern, the church of St Helena, a small campsite, a number of cottages

Devon Drizzle
The poet John Keats lived for a while in Teignmouth; like so many visitors he was frustrated by the weather:

Being agog to see some Devonshire, I would have taken a walk the first day, but the rain would not let me; and the second, but the rain would not let me; and the third, but the rain forbade it – Ditto 4 – ditto 5 – ditto – So I made up my mind to stop indoors, and catch a sight flying between the showers; and behold I saw a pretty valley – pretty cliffs, pretty brooks, pretty meadows, pretty trees, – the green is beautiful, as they say, and pity it is that it is amphibious – mais! but alas! the flowers here wait as naturally for the rain twice a day as the Mussels do for the Tide . . . This Devonshire is like Lydia Languish, very entertaining when it smiles, but cursedly subject to sympathetic moisture.

The average annual rainfall in Devon is about 40 inches, but there are large regional variations, the highest parts of Dartmoor receiving more than 80 inches whereas the Exe estuary has an average of only 30 inches.

The only solution is a good mackintosh and Wellington boots.

Thatch

The chocolate-box image of a Devon cottage, whitewashed cob under a thatched roof, is becoming increasingly rare. But today thatch is promoted and encouraged by planners and special grants to ensure that it continues.

Reeds, rushes, heathers and brackens have all been used in the past as 'thatch', but the rye, barley or wheat straw and water reed are the materials generally used.

Bunches of straw or reed are pinned to laths on the rafters with spars – staple-like pieces of hazel – and the ends are cut with a hook to a smooth finish, or butted level with a 'drift'. The ridge is often decorated with a thatched bird, animal or other symbol, the signature of the thatcher. The roof remains watertight because as the rain falls the moisture expands the layers of straw and they form an impenetrable layer so only the first two inches of an 18-inch-thick covering becomes wet, even in a fierce storm. Although eventually the thatch rots, a good roof will last up to seventy years, longer if very well cared for and repaired.

and two lighthouses, one at each end of the island.

In 1968 the Harmans, owners since 1925, decided to sell; Jack Hayward, a philanthropic millionaire, bought it and gave it to the National Trust.

In addition to the puffins, more than 400 different birds have been spotted, including the peregrine falcon, fulmar and curlew; Lundy was the last authoritative breeding place of the Great Auk (1841). Black rats live on Rat Island; deer, sheep, rabbits and the Lundy ponies occupy the main island. The flora is equally rich with wild flowers in abundance and the famous Lundy cabbage, *Brassicella Wrightii*, thought to be the ancestor of all mainland cabbage species.

Apart from looting, and a brief period of granite quarrying, the inhabitants have depended upon fishing for income and food; the thin, acid soil, and stormy weather makes arable farming a thankless task, but cows, sheep and poultry have adapted to the hardy conditions.

Day trips to Lundy are available from Bideford and Ilfracombe; those wishing for a longer stay should book through the Landmark Trust.

TORRINGTON

Inland north-west Devon is an area of small scattered settlements dotted through unspoilt countryside; there are no major towns, just a sprinkling of market centres and peaceful villages.

Torrington, or Great Torrington, seven miles south-east from Bideford, featured in the Devon Domesday book of 1086, indicative of its early importance as a strategic site. The town built on a prominent hilltop with precipitous drops to the south and west, overlooks the Torridge valley. It is not known when the first castle was built on the site, although records indicate one demolished in 1228, as it had been erected without a king's licence. In the 14th century Richard de Merton built extensive ramparts and a keep, and although nothing remains visible it is easy to imagine how imposing it must have been. The main road through the town, the A386, presents an aspect of dull terraces and plain houses, belying the character and interest of the town centre – Torrington is a busy friendly place, and its abundance of historical associations justify further exploration.

Entering the town from the Bideford direction, turn right down Whites Lane to South Street, where the car-park is well placed for a tour of the town. Leave from the farthest end of the car-park, where, from the ramparts of the former castle, the landscape spreads out in a patchwork of fields and hedges, and the river glistens far below. Follow the path to the left, where a slit in the wall affords a glimpse of one of the remaining parts of the castle. It is possible to walk for many miles along these paths – Torrington is surrounded by a horseshoe of common ground; but in order to see the town centre leave the path at the corner of the bowling green – reputed to be the site of the keep of the original castle. Some of the stone used in the construction of the present castellated walls was salvaged when they were built in 1846 by Lord Rolle. On the right down Castle Street, the Castle Hill Nursing Home, built in the late 18th century, was the home of the niece of Joshua Reynolds, who sat for him as a model for *Fortitude*. On the opposite side of the road a large stone set in the pavement marks what used to be the end of the borough.

The shops down Cornmarket Street and Potacre Street are small and traditional, and the architecture generally unspoilt. Turn left into New Street, where about 50yds on the right is Palmer House, an imposing town house of mellow stone, built in 1752, where

Thatching

Beaford Centre

Fire-eating, creative cookery and Arthurian legends all find a home at the Beaford Centre in north Devon; the centre was founded in 1966 as a satellite of the Dartington Hall Trust to serve the scattered rural population of the area.

Beaford has grown to become synonymous with touring theatre, experimental music, children's activities and other broadly cultural events that take place in village halls, pubs, car parks or wherever throughout the region.

It also acts as an umbrella organisation providing skills, materials and manpower to encourage community arts projects. In addition there are residential courses and short workshops on a great variety of subjects.

Housed at the Beaford Centre is a remarkable archive of photographs gathered from the surrounding area and recording all aspects of country life; they are supplemented by a modern collection taken by the Beaford's resident photographer.

Joshua Reynolds's sister lived.

Before entering the church, notice the rings set in the wall outside the churchyard, used to tether animals when the cattle market was held in the street. During the Civil War, General Fairfax took the town by surprise and captured the Royalist garrison; the prisoners were locked up in the church tower. By some terrible accident there was an explosion of gunpowder in the church which killed 200 men, and destroyed most of the building. The long mound by the churchyard path is said to be the mass grave, and there is an inscription commemorating the tragedy outside the porch. The church was rebuilt in 1651.

The church path emerges at the corner of Fore Street and the High Street. The town hall, with the clock, is carried over the pavement by stone pillars, and the cobbled floor leads through to the Shambles, once the meat market. Across the road from the town hall, in the Square, is the Black Horse Inn, believed to be the oldest building in Torrington; dating from the 15th century, its present façade is a result of rebuilding in 1681. The Pannier Market opens directly off the Square, through fine iron gates under the Market House (now the public library), dated 1842. At the southern end, past the market stalls, the town ends abruptly back at the Castle Hill beauty spot. On the north side of the town, down School Lane, is the Dartington Crystal Factory, where craftsmen demonstrate fascinating age-old techniques of glassblowing and the whole process can be watched from the safety of a viewing gallery. There is also a permanent exhibition tracing the history of glass and crystal over the past 300 years; a shop offering decanters, goblets, vases and ornaments, and a licensed restaurant.

Leaving Great Torrington south along the A386 over the river, bear left onto the B3220 signposted to Exeter. Just after the turn,

Rosemoor Gardens are in the care of the Royal Horticultural Society and are increasingly accessible and attractive, having been rather awkward to visit in the past. After about 5 miles the road enters the straggling village of **Beaford**.

The village is named after Berga, a Celtic chieftan who forded the Torridge and founded a settlement on the hill above.

The B3220 south from Beaford follows a high wide ridgeway between the rivers Taw and Torridge, with extensive views to the north and south as far as Dartmoor and beyond, unusual for Devon in that it is very straight and level, flanked by rough fields and occasional farmsteads and cottages. After about 9 miles is the town of Winkleigh.

Bypassed by extensive road-widening schemes on the B3220 during the Second World War, when an airport was built about two miles north of the town, **Winkleigh** remains unspoilt and untouched by the over enthusiasm of so many post-war small town planners. It retains the characteristics of a close-packed, clustered town in miniature, boasting a castle at either end, with the village tightly packed between; its half dozen shops are well scattered throughout. Park in Fore Street, which was the site of the original market, still displaying the old stone mounted pump 'erected by permission of the Lord of the Manor'. Winkleigh held borough status, with a market and fair, until 1848. The cottages and shops around the centre (Queen Street, High Street and Vine Street) are largely built of stone and cob, roughcast and colour washed. The town has two pubs, two banks, a charming restaurant, delicatessen and hotel, but is probably most renowned for the Wood-burning Stove Centre, with a huge variety of ranges and small heaters.

From narrow Dial Street, off Coopers Hill, cobbled steps lead up to the south porch of the parish church, which is mainly 14th- and 15th-century, with a richly carved and painted wagon roof. Notice also the 14th-century glass in the window at the west end of the north aisle, showing angels with the emblems of the crucifixion. The old Church House, under a neatly thatched roof, was built in 1536 at a cost of £28-14-4d. It has now been converted into two private houses.

Court Castle, beside the main road to the north of the village, forms a wooded knoll, with ivy-covered trees and rooks cawing in the ruins of the old tower. There is a smaller mound known as Croft Castle at the south-west end of Castle Street, behind the old Castle School. Both were probably in fact little more than moated manor houses, originating in the Norman period.

From Winkleigh to Hatherleigh is a well signed cross-country route of approximately 6 miles, via the small village of Monkokehampton. **Hatherleigh** lies 13 miles south of Great Torrington on the A386, an important market for agricultural produce and livestock, standing as it does on a major crossroads. The weekly influx of farming folk is well catered for by the nearby hostelries. The George Inn dates from the 15th century: it was originally a monk's residence, then converted to a coaching inn; the stone courtyard bears the traces of tracks left by the coaches as they rumbled under the archway; the place is well known for its good food advertised by a sign outside:

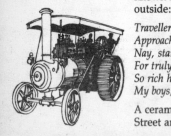

A steam engine at Alscott Farm Museum, Shebbear

Traveller, this inn which some call mean
Approach with awe: here lies a queen.
Nay, start not at so strange a thing
For truly she's a female King.
So rich her hashes, sauces, minces,
My boys, you here may live like princes.

A ceramic plaque at the junction of Bridge Street and High Street commemorates

Hatherleigh's 1,000 year anniversary, 981–1981; it illustrates the stepping stones of the town's progress: the bridge, the church, the market, industry and motor car. Named by the Saxons 'Haegporn Leah' meaning Hawthorn Glade, the town climbs the south-facing hillside above the River Lew, a tributary of the Torridge, surrounded by unspoilt vistas of pastoral north-Devon countryside.

The cottages are pink and white under thatched roofs, with walls askew and small-paned windows; the handful of shops in Market Street supply all the daily needs; on Bridge Street and Market Street are also a good selection of craft, antique and farm produce shops.

A few miles off the A3072 between Hatherleigh and Holsworthy is **Shebbear**, a scattered village, steeped in local traditions. Sometime before the Norman Conquest, Shebbear became the 'moot' or meeting place for the 'Hundred', the ancient administrative unit of 100 parishes; it was clearly an important place, with a small castle, in the north of the parish; many of the local farms were in existence by the 12th century. The oldest surviving buildings in the village itself were formerly the property of the parish and surround the old village green, now unfortunately asphalted; 'Scefbeara House', beside the churchyard, is a 16th-century Hall house and opposite, the Devil's Stone Inn was once the Church House, and has three dates set in its wall: 1645, 1678, and 1782. The cottages to the east of the green were the parish almshouses of the 17th century.

Returning to the A3072 turn west; after about 10 miles lies the town of **Holsworthy**. As a market town, Holsworthy comes alive, with a colourful display of stalls in the square and the cattle market bustling with people, and livestock, serving a far-reaching local community, and acting as the focal point for

The Shebbear Stone

Lying under a gnarled oak tree at the church lychgate in the village of Shebbear, is a great conglomerate stone, weighing over a ton; it is reputed to mark the site of the Saxon 'moot' or meeting place.

A local legend more imaginatively associates the stone with the Devil; it is said that he dropped the stone as he descended from Heaven to Hell, and that his bones now lie beneath it.

Whatever the origin, a highlight of the calendar is the Guy Fawkes Night ritual, when the bellringers create a discordant jangle on the church bells, and the stone is overturned with crowbars, 'to prevent the devil from getting his rest'.

During the First World War the ceremony was missed one year, and the following twelve months proved so disastrous for the village and many neighbouring farms that the locals have never dared to suggest breaking the tradition again.

day-to-day necessities for the numerous scattered villages in the area. Otherwise Holsworthy has little of great interest to offer; although some of the architecture is pleasing, there is none of exceptional quality. The triangular market place has a dull mixture of styles; mostly Victorian and modern, with an excess of hard red brick. Around the corner, Victoria Square is more intimate and attractive, flanked by shops and an excellent café; and here the buildings jostle together creating a haphazard skyline above the generally unspoilt façades. At the corner of Fry Street a plaque commemorates the Great Tree of Holsworthy, from which, by Royal Charter given in 1154, the annual July proclamation of St Peter's Fair is made. The parish church of St Peter and St Paul has a Norman niche in the porch, with a small Norman capital built in, and a carving of a lamb with a cross. Internally, the building has been subjected to much Victorian restoration, although the organ built by Renatus Harris, is particularly fine.

Dartmoor

6 Dartmoor

Covering an area of 365 square miles, Dartmoor is the most southerly National Park in Britain, and thanks to the hostility of the terrain and unpredictable climate, remains one of the most desolately beautiful areas in the country. Some 250 million years ago a great molten plug of granite forced its way from deep within the earth's crust, uplifting the layers of sedimentary rocks which overlay it. These softer rocks have been worn away, leaving the dome shaped mass of granite. Where it breaks through the surface it has been weathered and eroded into weird masses forming the characteristic tors. With fluctuating climatic conditions over the past 16,000 years accompanied by alternating dense vegetation and barrenness, peat beds were formed as the vegetation rotted and was compressed. These act as a huge sponge, absorbing the 60'' per annum rainfall and feeding the numerous rivers which radiate from the centre.

Only about half of Dartmoor consists of desolate 'high moor' however. The other half has charming wooded valleys, notably that of the Dart, and traditional rural communities such as Widecombe-in-the-Moor, which is well known, and Lustleigh, which is not.

Early evidence of human habitation abounds, largely on account of the durability of the granite used for building from the Neolithic period onwards. The movement of populations from hill tops to valleys in the Iron Age, as the climate deteriorated and tin was discovered in the river valleys, has meant that early sites have remained undisturbed by subsequent settlers, thus revealing a unique record of human activity. Tombs, hut circles, standing stones and reaves display the diversification of activity, also exhibited by later industrial remains from the medieval period to the late 19th century, when the natural resources of

Whortleberries
One delight of Dartmoor in July or August is chancing upon a crop of whortleberries – they grow in quantity, but are difficult to find. The berries are small and very deep blue or black when ripe, with a rich purple juice that stains the fingers; they grow in clusters, but are usually hidden beneath the foliage cover. The bushes are low and twiggy and from a distance they cannot be distinguished from heather.

Traditionally, whortleberry gathering – or 'pickin' hurts', in local dialect – was occasion for a holiday; the inhabitants of the moorland towns and villages took a day off to pick, heading for favourite spots in sheltered valleys where the berries grow in particular abundance. A hundred years ago, moorland families relied on a good picking to boost their income; berries fetched 6d (2½p) a quart at Tavistock market and on a good day it was possible to pick ten quarts.

It is hard to resist eating whortleberries fresh, particularly when sitting in a sunny hollow surrounded by bushes, but they can be baked in a tart or pie, or even fermented into a local brew known as 'hurt gin'.

tin, granite, and copper were extracted from the moor, leaving it pockmarked with redundant mine gulleys, tin streamworks, and buildings associated with the works. The agricultural importance of the moor developed from the Norman Conquest onwards, when the tradition of the Devon longhouse began, and early enclosures are still reflected by the boundaries of many farms today.

In the 19th century the moor began to be appreciated as a national asset, and visitors came to walk and benefit from the clear air. Concern that farmers were trying to over-exploit the natural wilderness, and growing interest from the Armed Forces for training purposes, led to the formation of the Dartmoor Preservation Association in 1883, which still exists and has to maintain the tenuous balance between the perpetual conflict of interests which determine the ultimate fate of Dartmoor. Today the landscape portrays a scattered population of isolated farmsteads scratching a living from the bleak moorland, and pockets of thatched granite cottages nestling in the lee of the hills. Although most industry has disappeared from the moor, traditional crafts and small cottage industries are enjoying a revival, spurred on by the increased tourist trade, now so essential to the maintenance, continuity and preservation of the moor.

BOVEY TRACEY

Bovey Tracey is an ancient market town and the gateway to Dartmoor. Though small, it is surprisingly well supplied with shops. There was a Saxon settlement here above the River Bofa or Bovey. After the Norman conquest the de Tracey family, from Traci near Bayeux, took over land in the neighbourhood. One Sir William de Tracey was amongst the party that murdered Thomas à Becket in Canterbury Cathedral in 1170; the rededication of the parish church to include St Thomas of

Canterbury, together with St Peter and St Paul, may suggest a substantial rebuilding of the church by Sir William as penance for his crime. In the 13th century Henry de Tracey created a borough and established the market. The present church dates from the 14th and 15th centuries – the carved screen, the stone pulpit and the font are particularly fine. The East Dartmoor Baptist Church in Hind Street is an impressive Georgian building in the Classical style.

Down by the bridge, the old mill has been converted to a permanent showroom and exhibition gallery for the Devon Guild of Craftsmen; the courtyard where millers' drays once rumbled over the stones is a pleasant open air extension to a restaurant. On the west side of the town, beyond the old railway station, Parke is the headquarters of the Dartmoor National Park Authority; the house and estate were left to the National Trust by Major Hole in 1974. Part of the grounds are used for a Rare Breeds Farm, but it is the woodland and riverside walks which are a sheer delight, especially in the spring.

Carrying on up the road from Parke, take the left-hand fork signposted Haytor and Widecombe. The road begins to wind steeply upwards; rough fields and isolated farmhouses nestling in sheltered hollows give way to open moorland, with scattered peripheral settlements such as Green Lane and Haytor Vale on the leeward side of the hills. Haytor itself is recognisable by being the first tor of any substance encountered on this road. The massive granite outcrops, like the twin humps of a camel, rise to 1,491ft. Steps have been cut in the rock to facilitate the ascent, but it remains quite a tricky climb. Views from the summit are impressive and extensive: the Teign estuary and the Channel beyond, and to the south the country spreads away towards Plymouth in the far distance.

Parke

About a mile west of the town centre of Bovey Tracey, Parke combines the headquarters of the Dartmoor National Park Authority with an information centre, craft shop, restored farm buildings, rare-breeds farm and woodland walks.

The rare-breeds farm, through the farmyard, exhibits a fascinating collection of poultry in the old walled vegetable garden of the house – feathery silkies, peafowl, ducks and geese; out in the fields are breeds of pigs, cattle, sheep and goats – most of them so tame and accustomed to visitors that they appear to enjoy the stroking hands of young visitors and fists full of grass proffered through the wire. There are rare Belted Welsh Black Cattle, with only 100 females still surviving; some of the breeds were common in the Middle Ages and can be traced back to prehistoric times.

Walks from the car park lead through the parkland and gardens of the house down to the valley of the River Bovey; it is a gentle path through mixed woodland and pasture, with the river clear, bright and swift, and tumbling over a weir – in the spring the daffodils are worth a visit.

Widecombe Church
One Sunday afternoon in October 1638, just as the Reverend George Lyde was delivering his sermon, a fiery thunderball rocketed through the congregation in Widecombe Church. It killed four people outright and several others died later from their injuries. When the survivors emerged it was found that the north-east pinnacle of the tower had been struck by lightning and fallen through the roof of the church. Local superstition ascribes the incident to a visit from Satan, who was tracking down a man in the village. On his arrival, he hitched his horse to the pinnacle of the church, and finding his victim asleep, dragged him to the top of the tower. In his hurry to get away, he dislodged the pinnacle into the church and vanished amidst the thunder and lightning.

The Widecombe schoolmaster at the time, Richard Hill, described the fateful day in a poem; a framed version of it can be seen in the church tower.

The road continues sweeping across the moorland, and after three miles begins the steep descent into **Widecombe-in-the-Moor**, perhaps the best known of all the Dartmoor villages, famed for its church, known as 'the Cathedral in the moor' and the song associated with its fair, held annually on the second Tuesday in September. The fair was once dominated by the sale of cattle, sheep and Dartmoor ponies, but is now heavily commercialised.

The village shelters in the valley of the East Webburn river, and is bounded by high, granite-strewn ridges, creating impressive Dartmoor skylines. Hameldown Beacon to the north, 1,697ft, was a beacon in Elizabethan times, and the moors around the village are scattered with evidence of past habitation. There are numerous hut circles, barrows and burial chambers dating from the Bronze Age, and at Foales Arrishes, about a mile south-east of the village, excavations have revealed Iron Age settlements.

In spite of its popularity and a preponderance of tea and gift shops, Widecombe remains undeniably attractive, with ancient thatched granite cottages clustered around the village green, or Butte Park, where the men practised archery after church – Butte being the old name for an arrow. The magnificent tower of St Pancras Church dominates the village – 135ft high and topped by four massive pinnacles, typical of the area. The tower, dating from the early 16th century, was funded largely by the local tin-mining community, and is somewhat later than the main body of the church, which is 14th-century. It was built as an alternative place of worship to the then 'parish church of the moor' at Lydford.

Internally the church is much larger than it appears, partly because the floor is below the level of the churchyard, and partly because the

Widecombe church tower

exterior is dwarfed by the tower. The barrel-vaulted nave has some finely carved bosses – notice the three rabbits above the communion rail, each with one ear, an alchemist's symbol connected with tin mining. The church house, built in 1500, was originally used as a resting place for visitors from farflung reaches of the parish, later divided into almshouses, used as a school, and now owned by the National Trust as a shop. The old smithy was in use until 1950, when it was preserved as a small museum, and just beyond it is an old Saxon well, outside the Vicarage gate, reputed never to run dry.

Leaving the village with the church on the left, follow the narrow road signposted to Buckland, Postbridge and Dartmeet, and a mile further on take the left turn to Buckland and Ashburton. This lane runs above the steeply wooded valley of the Webburn River. **Buckland** is a scattered hamlet, with some of the most picturesque cottages to be seen on Dartmoor, buried against the wooded hillside. The small church, built of local granite, perches near the hilltop. The only surviving remains of the original 12th-century building are the south door, the south wall of the nave and the fine font, carved with leaves and stars. Most of the work is 15th-century; the rood screen was probably the culminating piece of craftsmanship, with its unique depiction of figures outlined in black. Notice the clock face inscribed with *My dear mother* in place of numbers. It also chimes a children's hymn when it strikes.

As the road wends its way down the hillside, the landscape once again becomes more tamed as **Ashburton** is approached, a small country town of brogues and shooting sticks, set amongst the rolling hills in the valley of the little River Ashburn. The river tumbles through the town centre, to join the Dart below Dart Bridge.

Mine chimney near Ashburton

Templer Way
London Bridge, the National Gallery and the British Museum all began life, in part, as rocky outcrops in a quarry behind Haytor Rocks on the south-west edge of Dartmoor. It was the Templer family that organised the extraction of the stone and its transport to the sea.

Born to a poor Exeter family, the first James Templer (1722–82) made his fortune whilst in Madras with the East India Company. Returning to England, he married and bought Stoford Lodge, a dilapidated estate on the edge of Dartmoor, which included the right to quarry granite at Haytor. His eldest son James constructed the Stover Canal in 1790, which enabled easy transportation of the rich ball clay in the Bovey valley to the docks at Teignmouth, thus revitalising a dying industry.

George Templer, James' son, built a granite tramway, complete with tracks and points, linking his grandfather's quarries with the canal constructed by his father, to carry the granite to the sea. The tramway opened in 1820, but was in use for less than 40 years. Part of the tramway is still visible running across the moor behind Haytor, and together with the canal, which has been extensively restored, will eventually create a footpath linking Haytor to the docks at Teignmouth.

The origins of Ashburton go back to a Saxon settlement, perhaps an enclosure or market; a Portreeve was appointed by the King to oversee sales of property and cattle and to preside over the Court Leet, a judicial court. The tradition continues to the present day, when on the fourth Tuesday in November the officials gather at the Chapel of St Lawrence to be sworn in by the Court Crier, resplendent in colourful uniform. The chapel, now in the care of the Dartmoor National Park, was opened to visitors in 1988; the plasterwork is some of the finest in Devon, and there is a small exhibition telling the history of the building.

The town's prosperity relied on the tin and woollen trades. Ashburton became one of the four official stannary towns in Devon in 1285, where tin from Dartmoor mines could be weighed, and duty paid. The tinners and cloth manufacturers brought trade and merchants to the town, with the Ashburn powering a number of mills in the valley. Ashburton cloth was exported by the East India Company to China. The parish church of St Andrew reflects the medieval prosperity of the town: the church was almost totally rebuilt in the 15th century as clothiers vied with each other over the generosity of their gifts; at the base of the tower, the old parish chest is believed to have been made in 1483 by John Clyffe, a local carpenter, who received sixpence for his trouble.

Many of the vernacular slate-hung two- and three-storey town houses date from the town's heyday in the 17th and 18th centuries. The Market Hall in North Street, built in 1850, replaced a more picturesque 'shambles' at the Bullring; the ground floor was originally open and arcaded for dairy and fish stalls, and a pannier market at the rear; the arms of Lord Clinton, Lord of the Borough, are carved over the main entrance. Granite paving slabs are a feature of the town.

MORETONHAMPSTEAD

With Bovey Tracey, Okehampton and Ashburton, **Moretonhampstead** is one of the moorland gateway towns, developing as an important market centre for the north-eastern side of the moor, and catering for the farming communities in the settlements to the north. In recent years it has attracted a new range of small businesses, with potters, woodturners, shoemakers and artists establishing their crafts in the village.

Initial prosperity of the town was based on the woollen industry, and in 1207 it was granted a market charter and flourished until the wool trade began to decline in the late 17th century. It retained its importance, though, as a vital watering place for those negotiating the difficult terrain across the moor from Exeter to Newton Abbot. Unfortunately, much early architecture of merit was destroyed in a series of severe fires, but enough remains to reflect the early heritage of the settlement.

The main streets radiate from a central square, a design largely unaltered since the Middle Ages, although the village green has now been replaced by houses. The site of the parish church of St Andrew was used for religious purposes since Saxon times, the first stone building dating from the 12th century (several carved stones from this period are now displayed at the west end of the church). Most of the present church is 15th-century; the four-staged tower and staircase turret was completed in 1418. Past the church is the Sentry or Sanctuary Field; once part of the Glebe Lands it is now a public recreation area, with spectacular views.

Leaving the field by the gate on the right, walk up Cross Street where, immediately on the right, are the Almshouses, dated 1637, and unique in their construction. There is an 11-bay loggia with granite columns, above which are three tiny mullioned windows. Returning

Dartmoor Ponies
Descendants of the original feral Celtic ponies, long before the arrival of man ponies roamed Dartmoor in much greater numbers than today. Strong and hardy, they were well able to stand the harsh winters on the high ground. Originally used to draw light British chariots that charged the invading Roman legions, they were further domesticated and have been used for centuries as pack animals to carry tin, wool and peat across the moor and farmers rode them to tend stock or to pull carts to market.

The pure-bred pony stands 12.2 hands and is bay, black, brown or grey in colour, but they can only be seen at stud farms because the ones that roam the moor have all been cross-bred, usually with short-legged Shetland ponies so that they could work in the coal mines of Wales and northern England.

None of the remaining ponies are wild and they are rounded up every autumn by their owners to be sold as riding ponies or for slaughter; there is a large demand from the continent for small riding ponies, and the hardiness and intelligence of the Dartmoor has always ensured a popular and steady market. The moor could never support a large increase in numbers with its sparse pasture and competition from sheep and cattle. Apart from the annual round-up they spend the whole year on the moor in small herds led by a stallion.

One of Dartmoor's long-enduring traditions was the custom that if a house could be erected within just one day, between sunrise and sunset, then the right to stay in the property was established; the new residents also enjoyed rights to the common land for grazing sheep and cattle. Successful completion of the building was signalled by smoke rising from the hearth. However, the building had to be completed in secret, and should it be discovered during daylight hours then the punishment was banishment from Dartmoor and the house was destroyed.

The custom originated in the 12th century and continued until about 150 years ago when pressure from landowners prevented it.

During the 17th and 18th centuries there is no record of anyone succeeding in their attempt, but on Midsummer Day 1832, Tom and Sally Satterley became the last people ever to build a Dartmoor house in a day, and claim their rights. The house still stands, Jolly Lane Cott, near Hexworthy, between Two Bridges and Holne. On that day a fair was being held, so the couple hoped that everyone would be well occupied elsewhere. They had previously hidden beams for the roof and rushes for the thatch in the waist-high bracken, and collected stones that lay strewn around the moor. The house was very basic: a single storey, no windows and no chimney.

towards the town centre, notice the copperbeech tree on a granite-walled bed by the south gate to the church. This replaces an ancient elm, destroyed by a gale in 1891, known as the 'Dancing Tree'. So called, it was pollarded to create a punchbowl in the centre upon which a platform was placed on days of celebration, for performances to be given. The nearby rectory reflects the town's 18th-century prosperity. Further along Cross Street is Mearsdon Manor, for many centuries the most important house in Moreton. In about AD 700, Saxon settlers set up a farming settlement, occupied by a steward who managed the estate. The present building dates in part from 1309, when Sir Philip Courtenay enlarged and improved the Barton as his own Manor House. Externally, note the fine central granite chimney, a typical addition to more primitive structures. The main door is particularly splendid, as is the panelling of the screens passage. The building now houses an art gallery, tea rooms and brasswear and oriental crafts; a strange contrast to its origins, but at least rendering it accessible to the public.

Between Moreton and Bovey Tracey **Lustleigh**, about a mile from the main road, portrays Devon village life at near perfection, with thatched cottages clustered around the village green, delightful church, babbling stream, and village cricket ground.

Pleasant walks abound around Lustleigh and up nearby Lustleigh Cleave, a steep wooded valley gouged by the River Bovey.

Leaving Moretonhampstead in the opposite direction, follow the signs to Postbridge and Princetown, on the B3212. Two miles down this road, turn left for a quick detour to the charming village of **North Bovey**. Like Lustleigh, it epitomises traditional English village life, with cottages strewn around the green, flanked by oak trees and complete with old pump, and welcoming hostelry. Through the weathered lychgate lies the church, dating mainly from the 13th and 15th centuries, with an ancient font, and much notable woodwork.

Return to the B3212. The road twists through marginal farmland, eventually climbing out onto open moorland. The finest example of a prehistoric settlement on Dartmoor can be found at **Grimspound**, about a mile off the main road in a fold of the hills between Hameldown and Hookney Tor. A 9ft wide perimeter wall encloses 24 small round buildings within an area of about four acres. At the time it was inhabited in the early Bronze Age the climate was definitely more favourable, and the surrounding land would have been heavily wooded, but the relatively exposed position of the pound, with its numerous dwellings, meant that it was obviously not used for cultivation, but rather as a stock pen, although detailed knowledge of the inhabitants is still very largely a subject of conjecture.

The B3212 bisects Dartmoor, getting as near as is possible to the heart of the moor, and offering superb views in all directions, emphasising the expanse of the wilderness. At **Postbridge**, a small hamlet stretched along the highway, there is a well preserved medieval clapper bridge spanning the East Dart river. The huge slabs of granite, lain on stone piers, allowed easy access to pack animals, with no width restriction. There are good walks up the river, and also through Bellever Forest, and on to open moor beyond; the entrance is about ¼-mile further up the road.

Midway between Postbridge and Two Bridges is **Powder Mills**, once the site of a gunpowder factory, established in 1844 by George Frean. Its isolation enabled safe testing of the product without endangering neighbours, and the buildings were able to be well-spaced to reduce the risk of fire spreading. Some of the buildings have been restored, and

Dartmoor – Belted Galloway

Jay's Grave

A small unmarked grave lies just beside the road half a mile north of Houndtor. Unmarked, that is, except that it is always adorned with fresh flowers, and no one has ever seen who is responsible.

The Victorians' moral stand against illegitimacy condemned unmarried mothers to a life of degradation as social outcasts, below even paupers and thieves. It was dread and guilt that led a servant girl, Mary Jay, to take her own life.

She worked in a large household near Widecombe, and, having had an illicit affair with her master's student son, found she was pregnant. Unable to face the horrific consequences, she drowned herself in a shallow pool. When her body was discovered, she was duly buried, as were all suicides, in unconsecrated ground. From that day to this the mysterious flower-giver has never been revealed.

Dartmoor – raven

the Duchy of Cornwall sponsors various craft activities and a working forge.

Near **Two Bridges** is the ancient woodland of Wistman's Wood, which is of great interest to scientists but so fragile that visiting is not recommended. The genuinely interested must follow the signs. The wood may be one of the few remaining areas of natural Dartmoor Forest. The trees grow amongst the clutter of large boulders and debris from the tors, struggling to find a crevice for their roots. The resulting trees develop with gnarled trunks and branches, and they are covered with a thick coating of lichen, being 1300ft above sea level, well above the normal tree line for Dartmoor.

Beyond Two Bridges keep on the B3212 leading to **Princetown**. This is a grim granite town built largely at the end of the 18th century by Thomas Tyrwitt, who had extensive plans to transform what he saw as the wasteland of Dartmoor, by revolutionary scientific methods into a productive agricultural venture. Unfortunately, Tyrwitt had not fully appreciated the severity of the climate on this wild stretch of windswept moorland, and it did not take long for him to realise that his scheme would not sustain the settlement he had established. When the need arose for a suitable site for a prison to house first Napoleonic and later American prisoners of war, Tyrwitt proposed Princetown, and after approval from the Prince Regent, he laid the foundation stone himself in March 1806. It took three years to construct, and took the form of seven rectangular buildings radiating from a central yard like wheel spokes, each designed to house fifteen hundred men. Conditions were harsh, and rioting and epidemics commonplace.

The inmates were responsible for much local construction work, and the parish church of St Michael was built by them between 1810 and 1815. It is a drab edifice with unusually narrow aisles and square cut pillars, with the banners of those who served at the prison displayed at the west end. In the churchyard a tall granite cross serves as a memorial to all the prisoners who were buried in unmarked graves. Following the repatriation of the American prisoners in 1816, the prison remained empty for a period of thirty years, when it was reopened as a civil penitentiary.

Leave Princetown past the prison, and with the huge transmitter mast of North Hessary Tor on the left, take the B3357 back to Two Bridges. Keep on this road, signposted to **Dartmeet**, where the road drops down and the East and West Dart rivers meet in the steep wooded valley. A large car-park accommodates the hordes of visitors who flock to this beauty spot throughout the summer, but it is easily possible to escape the crowds by walking a short distance up or down the river, as few venture beyond the reach of the ubiquitous ice-cream van and public lavatories. Next to the road bridge are the remains of a storm damaged clapper bridge, which carried the packhorse track across the river before the construction of the Ashburton to Two Bridges road.

Although it is possible to return to Moreton across the moor via such villages as Widecombe and Manaton, for those without a good map it is easier to stick to the main roads, either returning on the B3212, or continuing beyond Dartmeet through Poundsgate and Holne Chase along the Dart valley to join the A38 at Ashburton.

OKEHAMPTON

The gentle landscape of north-west Devon meets the rugged upland of Dartmoor at **Okehampton**, with the two highest peaks of the moor, High Wilhays and Yes Tor, both over 2000ft within a few miles south of the town.

Tin Mining

In the Dark Ages ore was extracted by panning the alluvial streams, washing out and discarding lighter materials. Retaining walls and channels were often constructed to control the flow of water. Remains can be seen at Skit Bottom on the East Okement river, and at Brimbrook near Cranmere Pool.

The relict landscape of medieval mining, lumpy terrain of spoil heaps and pits, can be seen in many shallow valleys on the moors; the tinners built rough huts and furnaces for smelting the ore into ingots. Sometimes leats were built to harness water power for crushing the ore and to drive bellows for the furnaces.

As the alluvial beds were exhausted and technology improved, miners changed tactic and followed the lodes or seams of ore by digging gullies into hillsides as at Cater's Beam and Scudley Beam.

From the 16th century shaft mining was increasingly common. Gunpowder was used to break up the surrounding rock, and the surviving evidence of these mines is usually a gunpowder store, at a safe distance from the furnace and other buildings, housing machinery for lifting the ore to the surface. Evidence of such works can be seen at Eylesbarrow, and the East Vitifer shaft mine in North Bovey.

Okehampton

Population: 4,213

Early Closing: Wed

Market Day: Sat

Cashpoints: *Lloyds* Fore St; *Midland* 6 Fore St

Tourist Information: 3 West St (summer only)

Attractions: Museum of Dartmoor Life*, Okehampton Castle

Cinema: Carlton

By Road: London 197 miles (A30, M5, M4), Exeter 23 miles (A30), Plymouth 30 miles (A386)

By Rail: The nearest main-line station is at Exeter (2hrs 15mins from London)

With the completion of a long-awaited bypass, Okehampton now enjoys relative peace as the new A30, skirting the southern edge, takes the holiday traffic and juggernauts that once thundered through the town.

The original Saxon site was abandoned shortly before 1086, when Baldwin de Brionne, the Norman sheriff of Devon, favoured the present site on a wedge of land between the East and West Okement rivers; all that remains at the original settlement is the parish church of All Saints, which now stands solitary on the hillside away from the town. Built on the Saxon site, the granite tower dates from the 15th century, and the main body from 1843, although inside is a reputedly Saxon tombstone carved with a cross.

Because of the distance to the parish church, the Chapel of St James was built in the 12th century by Sir Reginald Courtenay, but once again suffered rebuilding in 1862, and is now of little interest, save for the fine 15th-century tower, which dominates the town centre. Further down Fore Street on the right is the recent Red Lion shopping precinct, which has attempted to retain a sense of individuality in its design, favouring a wide range of small locally run shops, with a traditional emphasis. The town hall, on the corner with Market Street, is an impressive three-storeyed building erected in 1685 as a town house by John Northmore, and converted to its present use in 1821.

Across the road an attractive granite archway leads to a cobbled courtyard flanked by two early 19th-century cottages and a three-storey agricultural mill and warehouse dated 1811, which have been converted and now house the Museum of Dartmoor Life and the Tourist Information Centre. The exhibits include archaeological finds and a geological display of the moor, together with descriptive reconstructions of local tin and copper mines.

More domestic paraphernalia is reflected in the Victorian cradle-to-grave display, and agriculture is traced from the numerous implements and wagons to an unusual 1922 Bullnose Morris with a wooden farm pickup back, and an ancient David Brown tractor. About a mile south-west of the town, Okehampton Castle commands a strategic site on a high knoll in the steep wooded valley of the West Okement. The impressive square keep dates from the Norman period, and towers above the remains of the Great Hall, buttery and kitchens (with its two ovens) which were rebuilt in about 1300.

Lydford, with its famous gorge and attractive village, is about 10 miles to the south-west of Okehampton, and well worth a detour. Leave the town on the Tavistock road, the A386, turning right where signposted to the village.

Although it is a relatively small settlement today, Lydford was originally established as part of a national defensive network to give protection against the Danes in the 10th century. It was the most westerly outpost of Wessex under Alfred the Great, and during the reign of Ethelred the Unready had its own Royal Mint. The town was never walled, but took advantage of its natural position on a promontory between the River Lyd and its tributary, and a huge earth rampart was built across the neck of land behind. Remains of the earthwork can be seen towards the north end of the village. Some of the town was destroyed by William the Conqueror as he swept in a trail of destruction across Britain, and soon after this a fort was built to the west of the church. This was short-lived, however, and the present castle dates from 1195.

The mound appears to have been raised around the castle at some later date – the reason for this is not known. Prisoners were held in the distinctly dank dungeons,

Hut Circles

Dotted over Dartmoor are the remains of hundreds of ancient hut circles, many marked on Ordnance Survey maps: these are prehistoric buildings dating from the Bronze Age. Some were dwellings, others stores or workshops. The best known and most easily visited site is at Grimspound, on the slopes of Hameldown near Widecombe, where a 'village' of 24 hut circles, varying in size from three to ten metres in diameter, is surrounded by an enclosure wall. It is a remarkably sophisticated site and a fertile imagination can conjure up the activity of the place.

Originally the walls of the hut circles would have stood a metre or more in height and timbers would have been laid from them to a central post – all supporting a conical roof of wood, turf, heather and bracken. Extra stability was sometimes given by an inner ring of posts.

Contemporary with the hut circles and demonstrating some complex division of the land is a network of low stone banks, called reaves, which stretch for miles, often in parallel lines, across moor and farmland. They can scarcely be seen from the ground, but aerial photographs taken after a light sprinkling of snow have revealed an extensive pattern of banks; they are thought to represent the potential arable territories of the various village dwellers.

Houndtor Village
Set in the shallow valley between the massive exposed granite castles of Hound Tor and Greator, half-hidden by the bracken and gorse, lie the remnants of a medieval village. The banks and enclosures, forming yards, gardens and small fields, surround a community of three or four dwellings, primitive versions of the Dartmoor longhouses, and various outbuildings and stores. Below is the deep but gentle wooded valley of the Becka Brook, and the mass of Haytor Rocks commands the opposite hillside. Rowan, thorn and oak have colonised the slopes.

The site was excavated in the 1960s, exposing low rubble granite walls, doorways, drains and hearths – all still clearly visible; the evidence discovered suggests that the village was built in the 13th century. Despite its exposed and relatively inhospitable position, in those days the climate was that much milder and fields were cultivated nearby with crops of oats and rye. At some point kilns, to dry corn, were built into some of the buildings and it is thought that this indicates a deterioration of the climate which eventually forced the inhabitants to leave; certainly the place was deserted by the mid-14th century.

whilst court sessions were held on the first floor. It became important as the seat of the stannary court and prison, dealing with the local tinners and anyone foolish enough to break the strict forest laws. From the front of the mound is an impressive view of Gorge House, an eccentric Rhine-like construction with twin turrets, built in the 1870s by a local wealthy curate, Reverend Chafry Chafry.

Next to the castle is the parish church of St Petrock. The original wooden structure was burnt down by the Danes, and the font is all that remains of the subsequent Norman building. The present church is mainly 14th and 15th century, with a low perpendicular tower with buttresses and crocketed pinnacles. Interesting features in the churchyard are the wheelwright's stone and the watchmaker's tomb. Access to the spectacular gorge is further down the valley, where the old stable block of Bridge House has been taken over by the National Trust. The gorge, 1½ miles long, has been scooped into a series of dramatic potholes as swirling boulders carried by the tumbling water gradually wear their way into the rock, creating features like the bubbling Devil's Cauldron, by Lydford Bridge. Visitors can walk along the picturesque wooded valley dripping with mosses and ferns, to the spectacular 100ft White Lady waterfall at the far end, or drive around to an alternative entrance. Be sure to wear stout shoes as the paths can be slippery.

To reach the pretty moorland village of **Belstone** take the A382 east of Okehampton, signposted to Moretonhampstead, and bear right shortly after the road crosses the new A30 dual carriageway. There is an abundance of typical granite architecture, cottages haphazardly strewn along the lanes and clustered around the church. Entering the village, notice the old stocks on the left, the attractive village green and the common, which leads directly on to the open moor. The small church of St Mary's was much restored in the 1880s, but the low tower is 15th-century, and it is worth visiting on a Sunday to hear the bells ringing across the moor. Belstone is an excellent starting point for numerous moorland walks, and there are interesting ancient remains in the vicinity. Near Belstone Tor, reached by following the lane to the west of the church, is a circle of standing stones, known as Nine Stones, although there are in fact sixteen. Local legend tells how sixteen maidens were turned to stone for dancing on the Sabbath, and they are reputed to dance when they hear the church bells. They are in fact a Bronze Age burial site. Also at Belstone Tor one of the famous Dartmoor Letter boxes can be found, complete with visitor's book and rubber stamp.

Follow the road back towards Okehampton, and turn right just before the edge of the village, signposted to Sticklepath and Skaigh. This picturesque narrow lane winds its way down Belstone Cleave in the Taw Valley, to the main road at **Sticklepath**. Originally a Saxon settlement, 'sticele', meaning steep, referred to the path that runs up the hill to the west. The village developed in the early 19th century as the water of the river was harnessed for power. At one time there were seven waterwheels, with a corn mill at one end of the village, the woollen serge factory at the other, and the Finch Foundry in the middle producing edge tools for agricultural use. This mill closed as recently as 1960, having been run by five successive generations of the Finch family. It has now been fully restored as the Finch Foundry Museum, with three waterwheels working a fascinating selection of machinery using belts, pulleys and hammers.

Continuing along the main road towards Moretonhampstead, bear left at Whiddon Down for **Drewsteignton**. Beyond the village, Fingle Bridge, a 16th-century bridge nestling deep in the wooded Teign valley, is an

William Crossing
Until the 19th century Dartmoor was viewed as a barren, dangerous wasteland of little value or interest; it was not until people like William Crossing drew attention to its wild and romantic beauty that the image began to change.

Born into a successful business family, he was made manager of his father's canvas mill at South Brent in 1847; but he never settled to the work and was constantly drawn to his beloved moor. He wrote poems and verses in praise of the landscape he loved.

Eventually the mill closed and he dedicated himself entirely to writing; he gathered an archive of information about Dartmoor, recording customs and traditions, folk memory and reminiscence. In 1901 he published *One Hundred Years on Dartmoor*; it was a great success but did not relieve the poverty that his business failures had brought about, and even when he published the definitive *Guide to Dartmoor* in 1909 he still relied on friends to support him. Gradually his exposure to the wind and rain brought on crippling arthritis, so he settled down to write a history of the moor.

Tragically, his housekeeper burned all his notes when she discovered mouse droppings on them and from then on his health declined and he spent the last few years of his life in Cross Park Hospital in Plymouth, where he died in 1928.

William Keble Martin
In the long tradition of parson and naturalist, Keble Martin produced the superb delicate watercolours for the bestselling *The Concise British Flora in Colour*, published in 1965 when he was eighty-eight. It is the result of a lifetime of study, whilst vicar of parishes throughout Devon.

Keble Martin obtained his degree in Botany and Theology from Cambridge University. He first came to Devon in 1921, to the living of Haccombe and Coffinswell near Torquay, where he designed a new church for Milber nearby. In 1934 he went to Torrington but found that the large and busy parish interfered with his botany and so returned to south Devon and the parish of Combe-in-Teignhead in 1943.

At seventy he resigned from the parish and retired to Gidleigh near Chagford to concentrate on drawing and painting the flowers and plants that were to become the illustrations in his book. When asked to explain the apparent conflict between traditional Christian belief and modern scientific botany he said, 'These two aspects of truth complete one another. We speak of natural law, let us call it the trustworthiness of nature, mercifully provided for us.'

excellent place from which to explore the riverside walks, returning for well-earned refreshment at the famous Anglers' Rest.

Retracing the road from Drewsteignton, turn left for nearby **Castle Drogo**, with spectacular views over the picturesque Teign Valley. Built on a rocky promontory, it is the last 'castle' to be completed in Britain. Designed by Sir Edwin Lutyens for Julius Drewe, it was constructed between 1910 and 1930. A massive granite structure, somewhat austere, it combines elements of traditional medieval castles with the more 'modern' requirements of its inhabitants, and is complete with its own telephone and hydro-electric system. The formal terraced gardens and croquet lawn (play available at a day's notice) offer magnificent views across the moor.

Carrying straight on across the main road at Sandy Park, the small moorland town of **Chagford** lies two miles to the south. 'Chag' is an old dialect name meaning 'gorse', and the ford refers to the crossing of the Teign, which was spanned by a bridge by 1224. The town nestles on the hillside above the river beneath rolling moorland hills, with fresh invigorating air and wafts of heather and sheep. In 1305 it was one of the original stannary towns to which tinners brought their metal for weighing and stamping, and Chagford bathed in the prosperity of the mines until the end of the 16th century. It continued to be an important market centre until 1831, but has gradually declined, although now much favoured as a holiday centre for those who want to explore the moor. The town is delightfully unspoilt, steeped in vernacular architecture, and an exploration on foot is essential. Park in the large car park by the Jubilee Hall, and cross the road to the fine 15th-century granite church of St Michael. The tragic death of Mary Whiddon at the altar in 1641 is said to have been the inspiration for Blackmore's *Lorna Doone*. In the churchyard is a medieval stone cross, which once stood in the market place.

Leave the church by the north gate into Southcombe Street and around the Square is a good selection of family-run shops, a small museum and art gallery. At the north end is an old granite trough used for watering the horses and cattle. The Market House, a six-sided granite building dated 1862, with pyramidal slate roof and spired lantern, is a focal point at the top of the Square. Crossing the High Street, and bearing left, the Three Crowns Hotel is a few yards on the right. It is a notable 16th-century building; the two-storeyed porch has the remains of seats and a cobbled pavement. It was the site of a skirmish in the Civil War, when the king's troops, led by Sir John Berkeley, attacked the village and clashed with some Cromwellian soldiers quartered at the Inn.

Adjoining the Three Crowns is what is now the British Legion Hall, but once the hall of the Guild of St Catherine, dating from 1200. The date stone of 1709 indicates probable repairs to the building following a great fire which damaged much of Chagford at the end of the 17th century. Next door again is an early-16th-century house, which was once the post office. Further exploration down the alleys and side streets reveals ancient granite cottages juxtaposed with grand 19th-century town houses.

Brentor

Perched precariously on the summit of a windswept tor 1100ft above sea level, St Michael's church claims to be the fourth smallest in the country. Its location is as inextricably linked with folklore and superstition as is the church itself with the rock on which it stands.

Construction of the first church at the bottom of the hill never got very far, as every night, legend has it, the building stones were mysteriously moved to the top of the tor. Constantly exasperated, the villagers eventually appealed to St Michael to rid them of this annoying interference and decided to build their church on the crown of the tor instead. St Michael, it is said, wrestled with the Devil (the anonymous mover of the stones) and overcame him, tossing him down the hill followed by a great boulder; the boulder is still there, as testimony. In fact the first church was built here about 1130 by Robert Giffard, the son of Lord de Longeville, one of William the Conqueror's knights; it was rebuilt at the end of the 13th century, the tower added a little later. As a chapelry of Tavistock, masses were held daily throughout the year.

St Michael's, Brentor

FURTHER READING

W. Crossing,
Dartmoor Worker,
David and Charles, Newton
Abbot, 1966

C. Gill (editor),
Dartmoor, a new study,
David and Charles, Newton
Abbot, 1970

W. G. Hoskins,
Devon,
David and Charles, 1954 (first
edition)

W. G. Hoskins,
Old Devon,
Pan, 1965

W. G. Hoskins,
Old Exeter,
1952

W. G. Hoskins,
Two Thousand Years in Exeter,
Phillimore, 1960

B. Little,
Portrait of Exeter,
Hale, 1983

A. Mee,
Devon,
Hodder and Stoughton, 1938 (first
edition)

Lady Rosalind Northcote,
*Devon – its Moorlands, Streams and
Coasts,*
Chatto and Windus, 1930